ANTONIO SANGIO

GUIDING
LOST SOULS

HELPING SPIRITS RETURN TO
THE LIGHT THROUGH HYPNOSIS

First Edition, 2021
Author's website: www.antoniosangio.com
Cover Design by Rob Williams
Interior Book Design by Antonio Revilla Leyva
Editors: Alejandra Travi Ponce, Juan Pablo León

ISBN: 978-1-7359669-6-0
Edited in Perú

*To my sons Tony, Christian, and
Sebastian, through whom I learned
love, patience, and compassion.
This book is for you.*

TABLE OF CONTENTS

INTRODUCTION

Explaining the Unexplainable

Many times, we do not need to see or touch something to know it exists. Since I came into this world, every minute, my lungs have breathed oxygen for me to survive. I cannot visualize it, yet I feel it inside me with every inhale and exhale. The same thing happened when I heard my mother's voice for the first time. In that instant, I discovered unconditional love without it really being tangible to me. Then, as I grew older and began to have my own thoughts, I instantly knew that they inhabited my mind without having to feel them.

How can we explain that which we can feel, but not see? From an early age, we have been asked to believe in things that we cannot verify with our five senses. For example, for a long time, religion demanded that I believe in a God I had never seen, just by observing his divine work around me. What is faith then, but to believe fervently in something that we cannot touch, but we can perceive in other ways. Today I am faced with the task and mission of revealing, transmitting, and sharing the love and help that I offer to those who, as I mentioned above, I cannot see nor prove that they exist, but I can feel.

This becomes even more difficult to understand because, even though I cannot visualize them, I communicate with them. I can feel their fears, anxieties, and pains, and unveil their stories and singularities.

I am referring to the spirits and lost souls—our spiritual brothers and sisters—who, over the years, have manifested themselves in different ways through my clients while in a trance.

In the path of regressive hypnosis, I have played different roles: that of student, practitioner, researcher, teacher, and, now lastly, that of communicator. Thus, I help to raise the level of human consciousness and open minds to other, more subtle dimensions.

The intention of this text is to share my work in assisting these spirits at all levels: whether they are lost souls, spirits of our loved ones, or those more advanced, whose mission is to guide us to the respective dimension of light.

I may never be able to prove scientifically what I will share in the following pages, nor do I think it is necessary in therapeutic work. My mission is to teach how to discover them (spirits), to understand them and, above all, to give them the love they need so that they can end their entrapment and continue their spiritual evolution.

***

Through the years of therapeutic work with regressive and spiritual hypnosis, I have encountered all kinds of situations. One of them is the origin of trauma in the human being, which causes part of one's energy to remain trapped in that painful event they experienced. This suggests that, at a subconscious level, when one goes through a similar scenario, they react in the same way as they did at the age when the trauma occurred.

Neither the subconscious nor the spirit understands time. For them, everything happens now. That is why, even though we may have gone through a traumatic event when we were only three years old, it may cause us, when facing a similar scenario, to react as we did at that age. It does not matter if we are forty, fifty, or sixty years old.

One characteristic of the conscious mind is that it protects us at all times. When it sees that some traumatic event may overload us, it encapsulates it and sends it to the subconscious mind to deal with it later when we are ready. However, not remembering an event that happened causes a void in our memory.

During my years of study, practice, and research in the field of hypnosis, I have learned different techniques to help my clients face those traumatic memories that are causing them problems now. On several occasions, those events had been generated through experiences in other bodies; that is, in past lives.

It didn't take long for me to realize that another reason for the appearance of those symptoms was the lost spirits attached to their vibratory field. These not only made my clients experience the same physical ailment the spirit felt before they died, but also transmitted their emotions, addictions, beliefs, and even suicidal thoughts (if this was the reason why their body died).

As I gained more experience in this field, I discovered that one of the most controversial, and most poorly researched and understood fields was, coincidentally, how to work with these lost spirits. Some of them had decided to stay in the house they lived in before they died, attach themselves to reincarnated spirits, or appear in the physical world to communicate something.

Unfortunately, some hypnosis techniques do not take these spirits into account; others mention them very superficially, while several refer to them— especially the lost ones—as demons, negative energies, or diabolical entities. Worse, when they communicate with them, they do it as if it were an exorcism. They insult them and use all kinds of adjectives while using the name of God to do so.

Quite apart from the ignorance and misinformation there is about these spirits and the therapeutic work with them, we can find the human fear of the unknown. It is this feeling that makes many therapists choose to close their eyes and pretend that this other consciousness attached to the vibratory field of their clients does not exist, causing these spirits to be completely ignored despite their attempts to dialogue.

In reality, it doesn't matter how much we know about hypnosis, how many techniques we have learned along the way, or how many clients we have served. If we do not know how to work with lost souls during a session, our therapeutic work will not be complete.

For example, if a person suffers from suffocation at certain times of the day and there is no medical solution for this, nor any traumatic event that could justify such a symptom, we should always be open to considering that this may be caused by an energy attached to their vibratory field. This was the case for a woman I received at my home for a hypnosis session. The asphyxia she was suffering from was caused by the soul of a young woman attached to her, who had died from suffocation in a fire in her village.

The motivation for writing this book has been to pass on the knowledge of my therapeutic work with lost souls and spirits over the years. I have not only helped my clients to understand the origin of their unexplained symptoms, but also those souls attached to them so that they can resolve the unfinished business that kept them from leaving and find their way to the light. In addition, it is essential for me to help society become aware of the importance of helping these wandering souls, who suffer without understanding what is happening to them.

We must know that a lost spirit deserves the same respect, time, and dedication that we give to the person who came to us for help. They deserve to be treated with love and compassion. Just remember that we are all sparks of the same universal light source: God.

I would like to end this introduction with an excerpt from the presentation made by Emmanuel, spiritual guide of the Brazilian medium Chico Xavier in the book *Workers of the Life Eternal*, psychographed and dictated by the spirit of André Luiz:

"How to transfer immediately to hell the miserable creature who became entangled in evil through the mere influence of ignorance? What will be given, in the name of divine wisdom, to primitive man, thirsting for domination and hunting? Damnation or the alphabet? Why lead to the dark abyss the least happy spirit, who only obtained contact with the truth right at the moment of abandoning the body? In the same reasoning, how to take to heaven, with determined character, the disciple of good, who barely started in the practice of virtue? What kind of task will characterize the movement of the redeemed souls, in the Heavenly Court? Would apostles be formed only for the obligatory retirement? How would be in paradise, the loving father, whose children have been delivered to Satan?"

I

DEFINING SPIRITUAL CONCEPTS

I think that, in order to understand what I am talking about when I refer to spirits in hypnosis sessions, it is important to understand what a spirit is, and what the soul and the ego are.

In the long run, we will realize that the definitions given to them in different cultures are basically labels to explain something that cannot be seen. In reality, we are talking about the greatest mysteries of humanity.

What is the Spirit?

The word spirit comes from the Latin *spiritus*, which means breath, and from the Greek word *pneûma*, which is related to the words breath, respiration, and spirit. The Greeks considered *pneûma as* the vital breath that animates the body.

This can be evidenced by going through the pages of the Bible, where the following definitions of the word spirit are found: wind, moving air, and breath. There, in Greek it is known as *pneuma*, in Hebrew as *ruah* and in Latin as *spiritus*; and the following references are made:

Genesis 2:7 7 then the Lord God formed the man of dust from the ground and breathed into his nostrils the breath of life, and the man became a living creature.

Job 34:14 If he should set his heart to it and gather to himself his spirit and his breath.

Psalm 104:29 When you hide your face, they are dismayed; when you take away their breath, they die and return to their dust.

In ancient Egypt, 'Ka' was regarded as a component of spirit, the universal and immortal principle of life; our life force.

According to the definition given in *The Spirits' Book*, which was written by Allan Kardec (Hippolyte Léon Denizard Rivail), based on a systematic communication with mediums, spirits are intelligent beings outside of creation who populate the universe outside of the material world. They are coated with a vaporous substance called perispirit, which allows them to rise in the atmosphere and transport themselves wherever they wish.

Throughout the history of mankind, different names have been assigned to something that in reality we cannot see or feel, and whose scientific demonstration is practically impossible. However, we know that it exists and that it is what gives life to the body.

It is enough to have witnessed the death of a loved one to see how, a few seconds after the death, the body looks and feels completely different. You can feel the absence of that spark of life that was there just seconds before.

For the purposes of this book and to help the reader have a better understanding of it, we will refer to the spirit as an energy field with an eternal identity with its own consciousness and intelligence, whose mission is to evolve through reincarnations in different bodies, or past lives. However, the truth is that, for the spirit, there is only one life, since it is immortal. For the spirit, time is not understood, since everything it experiences is experienced in the now. This means that, if the spirit had an experience in a past reincarnation in Ancient Egypt, for the spirit, it has just happened.

What is the Soul?

The word soul comes from the Latin *anima* and the Greek *psyché*. This first word refers to an entity, which, according to some religious and philosophical trends, all living beings possess. On the other hand, the second is a concept from the Ancient Greek worldview that refers to the vital force of each individual that is linked to his or her body and is released after death.

The Argentinean doctor José Luis Cabouli, creator of the Past Lives Therapy (TVP) method, says the following about the soul in his book *Terapia de la posesión espiritual (Therapy of Spiritual Possession)*, as I have translated:

In physical terms, the soul is a complex of electromagnetic and light fields that support the experience and manifestation of consciousness, the fundamental reality of our being.

Meanwhile, in *The Spirits' Book*, Allan Kardec shares the answer he got from mediums when he asked what the soul is:

What is the soul?

- An incarnate spirit.

What was the soul before its union with a body?

- A spirit.

Are souls and spirits therefore one and the same thing?

- Yes, souls are no more than spirits. Before uniting with a body, the soul is one of the intelligent beings who populate the invisible world, and it later temporarily assumes a physical envelope in order to purify and enlighten itself.

As we have been able to appreciate in the definitions mentioned above, although the soul has several meanings depending on the religious or philosophical aspect, they all agree that the soul is an intelligent being (energy) that occupies the body and that is detached from it when it dies.

As with the spirit, in this book we will refer to the soul as an embodied being of light and energy with its own consciousness and intelligence, that is, within the human body. But we will also use this name for the spirit itself, which when it disembodies and does not go to the light, maintains its ego, personality, and beliefs.

What is Ego?

The word ego, which comes from Latin and means 'I', has been adopted by psychology and philosophy to refer to our conscious mind. It is understood as our capacity to perceive reality.

The ego, therefore, concentrates the physical phenomena that exist between the reality of the external world, the ideals of the superego, and its instincts. Therefore, it makes us validate our opinion above the opinion of others, achieving that, automatically, we free ourselves from all responsibility in front of some event.

From my point of view, the ego is that part that constantly seeks to take care of us, trying to ensure at all times the survival of our physical body. It is coincidentally the ego that we should get rid of, both the therapist and the client, during a hypnosis session in order to be able to work on various traumas.

SPIRITUALITY

In the Merriam-Webster Dictionary, we find the following meanings for the word spirituality.

- Something that in ecclesiastical law belongs to the church or to a cleric as such
- Clergy
- Sensitivity or attachment to religious values
- The quality or state of being spiritual

The word spirituality derives from the Greek *voz spiritus*, which refers to the quality of spiritual matters or spirit. Actually, it does not have a single meaning. It can be understood as the search for meaning, transcendence, or the recognition of a universal connection.

In ancient cultures, spirituality was associated with gods and mythology, and the search for a psychic connection with the beyond; with other dimensions.

The Egyptians believed that all aspects of life were controlled by supernatural powers. They considered the universe to function according to a strict universal rule called 'Ma'at', meaning truth, balance, order, and harmony.

Spirituality, through religions, can be understood as the path in the search for transformation. While it is true that some may interpret spirituality as a set of doctrines and convictions, others understand it as the set of values of the human being. Let us not forget that spirituality exists with or without religion.

For me, spirituality is to understand that we are an eternal spirit with our own consciousness and intelligence, whose purpose is to evolve in love. It is to understand that we are spirits having a human experience in a school called planet Earth, where we come to experience and learn through emotions.

Spirituality means being aware that we ourselves, before we reincarnated, planned the situations we faced, are facing, and will face in the future. It is for that reason that we must take responsibility for those situations, understanding what our spirit thought we should learn from them when we planned them.

In addition, spirituality seeks to make us understand that we are part of a spiritual group, a kind of classroom with whose companions we will interact and play different roles from reincarnation to reincarnation. It means understanding that there are no bad or good beings, but beings more evolved than others. It is to feel love and compassion for others, helping them to get up and continue their journey, reminding them that we carry God within us, that spark of divine light from which we all come and which makes us one.

Spirituality also focuses on human beings conceiving that we are not victims of destiny, nor of other individuals, remembering that if today we have to play the role of victim, it is surely because in the past we played the role of the aggressor. Therefore, now it is our turn to feel in our own flesh what we made others feel. Nothing happens by chance. Even accidents are not accidents.

SPIRITISM

Since ancient times, man has believed in the possibility of contacting people who have passed away. In some cultures, shamans communicated with spirits in a trance-like state, while in others the dead and ancestors were venerated, based on love for them and a belief in their continued existence. They even believed that they could influence the fortune of the living.

However, if we talk about Spiritism, we must refer to its origin in the French doctrine Spiritisme, of the mid-nineteenth century, whose greatest proponent has been Allan Kardec, who in addition to publishing *The Spirits' Book*, also published *The Book on Mediums*.

It was Kardec who defined spiritualism as the science that studies the nature, origin, and destiny of spirits; in addition to the relationship of these with the physical world and the moral consequences of these links.

Spiritism is based on several concepts: the existence of God as a supreme and intelligent being and of spirits as individual beings created by God, the law of cause and effect (karma), the plurality of inhabited worlds—we are not only reincarnated on this planet—, the equality of spirits, and the belief that angels and demons are actually spirits with different levels of evolution.

Over the years, Spiritism has been practiced in other countries, where it has been divided into two currents: one as science and moral philosophy, and the other as science, philosophy, and religion, with Brazil being its base and Chico Xavier its greatest proponent.

Based on the definitions given above, we could then deduce that the difference between spirituality and spiritualism is that the former focuses on the spiritual development of the person, on evolution and connection with the universe and other dimensions, while the latter concept refers to communication with the spirits, with that individual intelligence and consciousness that we cannot see.

In this book, we will understand that, although in certain occasions we ourselves initiate a conversation with spirits through people in a trance state, there will be cases in which the dialogue will be spontaneous and originated by them.

This communication can have different objectives, such as giving us a message, resolving a conflict, understanding what prevents this spirit from moving forward, and helping it to become aware that its body has died and that it is manifesting through another body that does not belong to it. The fundamental thing is to help the spirit and the person to whose vibratory field it is attached.

SPIRITS IN ANCIENT CULTURES

Nowadays, there are several evidences that demonstrate the strong belief in life after death that several ancient civilizations had. They agreed that, in order for there to be life after death, the existence of some kind of substance or subtle body was necessary.

They also believed that the quality of *post-mortem* life depended directly on the type of life the individual had in the physical world, as well as the manner in which his or her body was preserved after death. Even, in many of these cultures, the manner in which the body was placed, the position in which it was buried, and the burial site were key.

Mesopotamia

In ancient Mesopotamia, located in what is now Iraq and the area bordering northeastern Syria, death was considered the last act of life, and from which there was no return. After death, the spirit went to what was known as *Irkalla* or 'the land of the dead', a large cavern located underground.

It was in Irkalla where the inhabitants were thought to continue a dark version of earthly life, where the only food was dust or dry earth. The ruler of the underworld was the goddess Ereshkigal, who lived in the Ganzir palace.

All spirits went to the same place after death. There it did not matter what they had done in life, for they were all treated in the same way. There was no judgment or evaluation of the deceased.

Ancient Egypt

Ancient Egyptian religious doctrines included three ideologies: belief in the underworld, in eternal life, and in the rebirth of the spirit.

The concept of eternal life was generally seen as an indefinite rebirth. Therefore, upon death, spirits were guided to Osiris to be born again. The Egyptians had a series of burial rituals, considered necessary to ensure the immortality of the soul.

They believed that the human personality had several facets and that the person was, in reality, a complete entity. Depending on the person's development, they could use different forms after death to assist those they wished to assist and even to take revenge on their enemies. Among these forms were the following:

- Khet was the physical form that the spirit needed to possess intelligence or to be able to be judged by the guardians of the underworld. For this reason, the corpse had to be preserved as carefully as possible.

- Sah was the spiritual body that allowed interaction with different entities in the afterlife. It was believed to allow the spirit to return to take revenge on those who had wronged them in life.

- Ib, or the heart, was the nexus for emotion, thought, desire, and intention. In Egypt, the heart was the key to the afterlife, a fundamental part of the judgment that the spirit would face. Therefore, this organ had to be preserved as well as possible inside the mummified body.

- Ka was the concept of the vital essence, the difference between a living or dead person. Death occurred when the Ka left the body.

- Ba was personality; what made a person unique.

- Shut was the shadow that is always present and contains part of the person.

- Sekhem was the form, the life force that exists in the afterlife once the judgment has passed.

- Ren was the name. As part of the soul, Ren was given to human beings at birth. It was believed that they would live as long as their name was pronounced.
- Akh was the intellect and was understood as a living entity.

Ancient Greece

In Ancient Greece, when a person died, a coin was placed in the mouth of the deceased as payment to Charon, the son of Erebus and Nyx, whose function was to transport the spirits along the rivers Styx and Acheron after having received the funeral rituals.

Once the spirit was on the other side, he would meet Cerberus, the three-headed dog that guarded the portal to the underworld; then he would go to the judges and give an account of the decisions he made in life.

The final destination of the spirit depended on this judgment. A few went to the Elysian Fields, some to the Asphodel Meadows, and others ended up in the darkness of Tartarus. No spirit was condemned for all eternity.

Ancient China

In this civilization, considered one of the oldest in the world, life after death was believed to be a kind of journey across a bridge to the afterlife. Spirits were judged as worthy or unworthy during this odyssey. If they had done good deeds, they could continue the journey, but if they had done evil, they fell off the bridge into hell.

A proper burial was of great importance at that time. The land beneath the ground was considered the property of the gods, and a grave could not be dug without first honoring them and 'buying' that area from them.

In addition, the spirit was thought to consist of two parts: the 'po' and the 'hun'. The former was associated with darkness, water, and earth, and the latter with light, fire, and the heavens.

Mayan Culture

For the Maya, life and death were indispensable complements. They believed that death was not the final destination. Therefore, in their tombs, they placed food in the form of offerings for their journey after death. Depending on the hierarchy and prestige of the deceased, it was possible to sacrifice female servants to accompany them on their journey.

Preparation of the body could include placing ground corn in the mouth along with a drink they called 'koyem'.

The Maya conception of life after death is similar to that of Mesopotamia, where the underworld was considered a dark and terrible place. In the Maya underworld, also called Xibalba or Metnal, there were lords of death who could deceive the spirit, who was in search of paradise.

Once the spirit descended to the underworld, there was no return.

The Incas

The Andean-Inca worldview saw nature, man, and Mother Earth (Pachamama in Quechua) as a whole. Under this worldview, man, animals, plants, and mountains all have a soul; a vital force.

The Inca Empire believed that the world had three planes:

- Uku Pacha: underworld or world of the dead.
- Kay Pacha: the world of the present and the here, where living beings spend their lives.
- Hanan Pacha: the world above, celestial or supraterrestrial, where only righteous people could enter by crossing a bridge made of hair. This was the world where gods such as Viracocha, Inti, Mama Quilla, Pachacamac, and Mama Cocha, among others, lived.

The Incas believed in the continuation of life after death. It was for this reason that they buried their deceased in fetal position inside funerary bundles, recreating the maternal womb to initiate the process of rebirth, since they believed in reincarnation.

According to the writings of Felipe Guamán Poma de Ayala, an Amerindian chronicler of Inca descent, the process of preparing the corpse included dressing it with the best clothes and accessories, accompanying it with the products it liked the most in life. Depending on the social status, some gold and silver objects were placed in the tombs. Gold represented the sun and silver the moon.

***

Although I have only mentioned a few of the many cultures that have existed in ancient times, it is easy to find a common denominator in them: the belief in life after death and the process through which a spirit goes through from the moment it leaves its body, going through a stage of judgment or evaluation of its earthly experience, and then arriving at a final destination according to how it lived that life.

Other cultures that also believed in life after death were the Aztecs (Mexico), the Maori (New Zealand), the ancient Romans, the Celts (Central Europe), the American Indians (United States) and the Vikings (Scandinavia).

Some ancient civilizations and some religions today have handled the concept of heaven and hell. The first is considered a place or higher plane, a kind of paradise that has been known by different names such as: the seven heavens, pure lands, Tian, Jannah, Valhalla, among others. The second is considered by many religions and cultures as the place of torment and punishment after death. It is believed that this site is located in another dimension, below the earth's surface. In addition, other *post-mortem* destinations have been mentioned, such as limbo and purgatory.

It is surprising that, despite being separated by vast territories and oceans, so many ancient cultures share the same beliefs and descriptions of the journey of the spirit after death. How could their ideas and principles be so similar? What led them to believe that the spirit follows a new path after leaving its physical body?

SPIRITS AND SHAMANISM

Since time immemorial, human beings have believed in the existence of a parallel world inhabited by disembodied beings with their own consciousness and intelligence. These beings are asked for favors and help, but are also believed to be the cause of physical, emotional, and psychological illnesses.

In different cultures, territories, and languages, it is believed that there were and still are people with extrasensory gifts and extensive knowledge about nature, who seek contact with these beings to alleviate the sorrows of these sick individuals. They are considered a kind of doctors and experts in the field, and are known as shamans.

The word shaman refers to the healers of Turkey and Mongolia, in north-central Asia (Siberia). Shaman means doctor in Turkish and is the equivalent of the *medicine man* of the Indian tribes of North America, where they arrived from Siberia.

Shamanism is understood as a kind of belief and practice inherited from ancient cultures, which claims to be able to diagnose and cure different ailments and sufferings of human beings through shamans and their connection with the spirit world.

In addition, shamanism is considered one of the most primitive forms of establishing communication with spirits. It is based on the premise that the world is plagued by these invisible entities, who inhabit a dimension parallel to ours, coexisting with it and affecting it in different ways.

Shamanism believes that spirits can be good or evil, and that the shaman can heal illnesses generated by evil spirits through trance-inducing techniques to obtain visions.

Shamans may have the following skills:

- Communication with more subtle worlds.
- Assistance from one or more spirits, and may even have an animal spirit as a guardian.
- Mental gifts, such as being intuitive and sensitive.
- Direct communication with spirits through the hypnotic trance state.

Although shamanism believes that illnesses are caused by evil spirits from the spirit world, the shaman uses both physical and spiritual methods to heal. Sometimes, in a trance state, they enter the patient's body to confront the spirit that causes the ailment. Because some have excellent knowledge of local medicinal plants, they may prescribe a regimen of herbs as treatment.

The shaman not only uses hypnotic trances to access the other dimension or spirit world. They also use tools and methods, such as tobacco smoke, the beat of a drum, fire, dances, icaros (medicinal songs), and vigils, among others.

In some regions of South America, shamans are also called healers. In the Inca Empire, called Tawantinsuyo, they were known as Willac Umu (high priest in Quechua) and were distinguished by their knowledge of medicine, religion, and astronomy. They had excellent control in communicating with spirits, which could enter them to help others suffering from physical-psychic or psychosomatic problems.

In Korea, shamanism is called Muism and is completely linked to the figure of the shaman and their role as a bridge between heaven and earth. In this region, people who still practice this traditional religion perform shamanic rituals to eliminate the resentment felt by the deceased towards the world of the living. Among the ceremonies to guide the spirits to the underworld is the 'cheondogut', which is officiated by a professional who plays the role of intermediary between the world of the gods and the world of the living.

In the Mayan culture, shamans had a very important role since they were considered the direct connection between mankind and gods. They were the ones who advised different healing methods in a time when western medicine did not exist. Thus, through the use of plants with hallucinogenic effects, they sought to separate the body from the spirit, in order to have a vision of other, more subtle planes or other dimensions.

SACRED PLANTS

Since ancient times, humans have used plants with hallucinogenic effects, both to heal illnesses and to enter into a state of expanded consciousness in order to contact other dimensions and the spirits that inhabit them, be they advanced beings of light or their own ancestors.

Many believe that medicinal plants fulfill the same function as sacred plants, but this is not so. Medicinal plants, which can be thousands around the world, are those that have healing powers. On the other hand, sacred plants are those that, besides being curative, have the characteristic of being psychoactive and of being able to take the one who consumes them to expanded states of consciousness; to a kind of hypnotic or mystical trance.

The use of sacred plants is not alien to the shaman, who have a wide domain and knowledge about them. These, in general, act on the central nervous system causing changes in its functions.

However, for the experience to be favorable, the person must have a correct intention and must know how to use the plant. Unlike hypnosis, the sacred plants induce us to a state over which we have no control and which will last until its effect ends, which means that we have no power over the whole experience. If, for some reason, what we are feeling is not what we desired or is simply not to our liking, we will unfortunately have to endure the whole experience.

Another key point to consider is that when we are in an altered state of consciousness, our spirit leaves our body, becoming unprotected and exposed to other spirits or lost souls that may take advantage of the opportunity and attach themselves to our vibratory field.

Not all experiences are bad or dangerous, as I know of many that turned out to be highly positive for the individual. However, I will always recommend researching and getting to know the shaman who will be in charge of guiding and taking care of you, because, unfortunately, ambition has ended up corrupting the millenary plants used by our ancestors. Nowadays, it is very common to come across people on the Internet offering individual or group ceremonies without any real knowledge of the plants and their impact on the human being.

Another thing I advise is to be very clear about our intention: "What do I need to get from this experience? What do I need it for?" It is also important to choose the right people to accompany us, and an optimal and harmonious place because, as we will see later, there are certain spaces and individuals that act as great repositories of lost souls.

Personally, I have witnessed hypnosis sessions where people related how, during an ayahuasca ceremony, their soul left their body while energetic parasites entered it without them being able to do anything about it.

There is a great diversity of sacred vegetation, but I have chosen only three botanical preparations to discuss. Some of these produce what is called 'a small death', which helps the spirit to leave the body in search of other dimensions.

Ayahuasca and Chacruna

The Quechua word ayahuasca means 'rope of the dead' or 'vine of the spirits', and is considered a bridge between the physical world and the spiritual world, between health and illness, between life and death. It is a huge climbing plant with vines up to 30 meters long.

Cooking this plant in hot water together with the chacruna shrub results in a powerful drink also called ayahuasca or yagé. This, when ingested, increases the amount of DMT (Dimethyltryptamine) that we all have in the pineal gland, producing physical and cerebral effects that lead the individual to experience an altered state of consciousness. According to some studies, this is not a hallucinogen or a drug, but note that several countries classify it as such.

Used by the Amazonian peoples of Bolivia, Brazil, Colombia, Ecuador, and Peru; ayahuasca and chacruna are considered master plants that are mostly used to work on ourselves, as we explore the labyrinths of our mind and open our spirit to other realities. However, it is not uncommon during this out-of-body experience to be shown past lives or to have contact with spirits that come to help us or provide us with information.

Sacred Mushrooms, Flesh of the Gods

Also called magic mushrooms, these organisms belong to the psychoactive species. Their use is widely documented in Central America, especially by the Aztecs, who used to consume them for sacred purposes. Its name is teonanácatl, which means 'flesh of the gods'.

When consumed, they caused hallucinations and visions of the deities they worshipped.

San Pedro

Also known as 'wachuma' or 'huachuma', it is a psychoactive cactus species currently used by indigenous people from Peru, Bolivia, and Ecuador. This cactus contains mescaline, an alkaloid with hallucinogenic properties.

In curanderismo sessions in northern Peru, it is customary to drink a concoction called 'the remedy', whose main ingredient is the pulp of the San Pedro. This drink is ingested by the attendees of curanderismo sessions, which are guided by shamans, with the purpose of being in an altered state of consciousness during the ceremony, facilitating the work to be done on themselves.

Shamans claim that this substance allows them to perceive what is invisible to the naked eye, so they can connect with the spirits in that dimension and ask them for help and information.

***

From what has been described above, we can see that human beings have been searching for contact with other dimensions and with the spirits that reside there for many years. The motives are really diverse, but they all agree in the desire to find answers to their questions, heal their illnesses, find protection, receive advice, and even reconnect with an ancestor from whom they need some information.

While it is true that we all have the ability to connect with these spirits and dimensions, on many occasions we turn to people who have extensive knowledge on the subject to serve as intermediaries. We are talking about shamans, who play the role of bridge between the physical and spiritual world to achieve these purposes.

Another way in which human beings have achieved this connection has been through the use of plants considered sacred. As we just discussed, these possess psychoactive and hallucinogenic agents that take the individual to a state of expanded consciousness in order to achieve the much-desired communication.

Nowadays, it is possible to recreate that state in other ways. Meditation is one of them, but the most effective and well known is hypnosis, among which are regressive and spiritual hypnosis.

Although, recently, the use of hypnosis has reached great diffusion, the truth is that it has been used since ancient times, when it was not even known by that name. If we go back to ancient Egypt, about 4,000 years ago, we find the temples of sleep or dream temples, under the rule of Imhotep, high priest of the sun god Ra in Heliopolis. These spaces were a kind of hospital dedicated to the treatment of ailments of psychological origin. The procedures included chanting, placing the patient in a trance state, and analyzing their dreams to determine the treatment to be followed.

DEATH ACCORDING TO RELIGIONS AND DOCTRINES

Buddhism

Like other religions, Buddhism believes in reincarnation, that is, in returning to Earth in another physical body after the death of the present body. This original Indian philosophical and spiritual doctrine comprises a variety of traditions, religious beliefs, and spiritual practices mainly attributed to the sage and hermit Gautama Buddha.

For Buddhism, the quality of life in a future reincarnation will depend on the quality of life we are leading now, that is, our current actions will directly influence how we will live in the body we have in the future. This is also known as dharma (actions done for good) and karma (the consequence of what has been done). In other words, it is about the laws of cause and effect.

A Buddhist's intention is to achieve constant evolution throughout the reincarnations in order to attain enlightenment. Two fundamental goals for this are: liberation from Samsara (*Samsāra* in Sanskrit), which is the cycle of birth, life, death, and reincarnation; and, enlightenment, which turns the individual into a Buddha.

Buddhism believes that a subtle mind and body can store the karmic information of all our physical, mental, and verbal actions performed from reincarnation to reincarnation. According to this religion, the level of consciousness in which a person is moments before death is of utmost importance. It is for this purpose that the Mahayana tradition has developed chants, rituals, and processes to help the body to have a more propitious transition.

In Buddhist countries that practice Mahayana, someone must whisper the Buddha's name into the ear of the person who is about to die or who has just died, so that this is the last thing he or she hears. The body is then placed in a coffin surrounded by floral wreaths and candles, and the funeral may take place days after death to allow the first state of 'bardo', a state of existence between two lives on Earth, to take place.

In Tibet, a country where Mahayana is prevalent, a detailed guide is read to the spirit of the deceased 49 days after death. In the case of Tibetan Buddhists, this text is *The Tibetan Book of the Dead*. It is said that, during this period, the spirit goes through a series of confusing intermediate states and is able to be influenced by other spirits.

Christianity

The Christian religion considers death as one of the consequences of the original sin inherited from Adam. On this subject, the following can be found in the Bible:

Romans 5:12 Therefore, just as sin came into the world through one man, and death through sin, and so death spread to all men because all sinned—

Romans 6:23 For the wages of sin is death, but the free gift of God is eternal life in Christ Jesus our Lord.

Christians believe that death is the separation of the soul (the breath of life, *psyche*) from the physical body, so that the spirit can then return to God. In the Bible, it is said that, after physical death, believers are taken by angels to the creator.

Luke 16:22 The poor man died and was carried by the angels to Abraham's side. The rich man also died and was buried.

Luke 16:23 And in Hades, being in torment, he lifted up his eyes and saw Abraham far off and Lazarus at his side.

The Bible also mentions that Jesus Christ will return to Earth and judge all men; the unjust being consigned to hell, a place of eternal punishment.

Christian burial rituals include the wake, where the body is prepared by washing, wrapping, or dressing it; viewing or vigil of the corpse; religious service, where Bible readings, psalms, and prayers are read, and the coffin is carried from the church to the cemetery; and graveside service, where a priest commends the body to the earth with the phrase "ashes to ashes, dust to dust".

Islam

Islam considers death as a transfer or a life in another dimension, where the spirit lives beyond the body. In other words, this religion, founded by the prophet Mohammed, believes in a continuity of life, in an intermediate phase between death and the day of resurrection or final judgment.

It is believed that we are all born with a purpose to be fulfilled before death: to worship Allah, the one true God, on his terms and conditions.

Noble Quran 51:56 And I did not create the jinn and mankind except to worship Me.

Noble Quran 29:57 Every soul shall have a taste of death in the end to Us shall ye be brought back.

Islam also maintains its own conception of paradise and hell, destinations to which souls go as a consequence of their actions after the final judgment.

As for mortuary rituals, like Judaism, Islam forbids anything other than burying the corpse underground. The body is treated with a ritual cleansing and then wrapped in a white cloth without knots so that the soul is not prevented from leaving. Once this is done, the burial proceeds in the absence of coffins.

According to tradition, once the corpse is buried and in the absence of the relatives, the angels will raise the soul. But, before accompanying him to rest, they will ask him five questions: who is your God, who is your prophet, what is your holy book, who is your imam (religious leadership position), and what is your *qibla* (prayer direction)? If the answers are: Allah, Muhammad, the Quran, the name of the imam, and Mecca, then the soul will find its peace in burial.

The Spiritism Doctrine

Although it is true that in some parts of the world spiritism is treated as a kind of religion, we cannot affirm that it is because it does not have dogmas, cults, rituals, hierarchies, and it does not ask for blind faith. Spiritism is, in reality, a philosophical doctrine with religious consequences since it necessarily touches the bases of all religion: God, life, the soul, and the future life.

To give a better explanation of what happens at the moment of death, it would be good to refer to the description given in the book *The Messengers*, channeled by the famous Brazilian medium Francisco Cándido Xavier (Chico Xavier), whose additional author was André Luiz, who in turn was a famous doctor in his last life. It should be noted that the explanation given by him was made from the spiritual world, from a more subtle dimension invisible to us.

There, Luiz describes the spiritual assistance given to Fernando, a man in his sixties who had been in a coma for a few days. In the book, he tells how a kind of magnetic passes were used to achieve the final separation from the body and details how disembodied spirits were present in Fernando's room in order to help him. Among these spirits was that of his mother.

It is essential to emphasize that the reincarnated relatives, who were also in the room with Fernando and felt a great affliction for his condition, emitted a kind of magnetic net over his spirit, making his detachment more difficult. Fernando's assistance ended when it was cut. He describes that sensation as something like an umbilical cord—perhaps what we know as the silver cord—being cut, thus achieving complete separation from the body to proceed to be accompanied into the light by the spirits that had been assisting him.

On the other hand, in the book *Workers of the Life Eternal* by the same author and also dictated by André Luiz, there is a detailed description of the spiritual assistance given to Dimas during his disincarnation.

Here he explains how Dimas' energy was gradually separated from the body until it formed a kind of parallel energetic body, which was still attached to the physical body by the same cord referred to above. What is interesting in this case, even though Dimas' physical body had already died, is that the spirits assisting him left the energetic body attached to it until the next day, because it was not prepared for a quicker separation.

How many times have we heard dying people tell us that they are visited by people who have already passed away? The truth is that, during the process of death—of the detachment of the spirit from the physical body—the dying person gradually gains access to the other dimension. That is why it is not unusual for them to say that deceased beings are coming for them, since what is really happening is that these spirits are coming to assist them in the final detachment.

If I refer to my own experience, perhaps I could tell about the moments prior to the death of my father, who, although he did not experience a prolonged agony, I am sure had a process very similar to the one described by André Luiz.

Two days before his death, he was able to see my uncles (the spirits of his deceased siblings) come to visit him and greeted them with great surprise. Also, as I watched the life in his body slowly fade away, I could notice how on the last day he felt practically no pain. Every time I asked if he wanted me to give him the pill he was taking for pain, he told me it was not necessary. My only explanation for this is that he was already being assisted and was slowly being disconnected from his body.

His room, which had always been characterized as warm and even more so during the summer season, was cold on his last day of life. I felt and knew that this change in temperature was due to the presence of the spirits that were assisting him.

The funny thing is that even his cat realized the same thing, when from one moment to the next, she gave a meow that made him jump with fright as she passed by the foot of my father's bed.

THE TIMELESSNESS OF THE SOUL

To talk about the timelessness of the soul, what this means, and how it is affected or how it functions within this concept, I think we should first define what time is; at least what we, reincarnated spirits living in the third dimension, understand as time.

What is Time?

Time can be understood as a physical magnitude with which the duration or separation between events is measured. To the human brain, time is linear, that is, with a sequence and order: present, past, and future.

According to the systems theory proposed by the German sociologist Niklas Luhman, time has a social formation, that is, it is situated from the perspective of the observer, who concretely makes a distinction of a before and an after. The before is the past, the after is the future, and the midpoint between the two is the present in which the synchronization of simultaneity is found.

Quantum time, on the other hand, is where a person unfolds in a state of hypnotic trance. I am referring to the time existing in the subtlest dimensions, where incorporeal beings dwell.

The Illusion of Time

Humans are used to seeing time as a constant, but the renowned German physicist Albert Einstein proved that it is actually just an illusion. It can speed up and slow down, depending on our speed through space. An example of this is the fact that astronauts age slower when they are in outer space.

For Carlo Rovelli, Italian physicist and author of *The Order of Time*, to understand the common concept of time is to accept that it has several layers. He argues that confusion in trying to understand its meaning is generated when we take all its attributes as a single package, as a whole, when in fact many of the properties and attributes of time come from mere approximations and implications.

In quantum time, the present, past, and future merge into the now. According to the properties of the quantum universe, elementary particles of matter can be in two different places or states at the same time.

For example, the Copenhagen Interpretation theory, formulated in 1927 by the Danish physicist Niels Bohr with the help of Max Born and Werner Heisenberg, holds that a particle remains in superposition or in different places at the same time until such time as it is interacted with or observed by the outside world.

In 1935, Austrian physicist Erwin Schrödinger created an imaginary example to understand this theory, where a cat, a vial of poison, and a radioactive source are placed in a sealed box. If an internal monitor detected radio activity, the vial would break, releasing the poison that would kill the cat. In the Copenhagen Interpretation of quantum mechanics, Schrödinger's cat is in a quantum superposition state of being alive and dead at the same time and, just by opening the box and looking at the cat, it would become one or the other.

On the other hand, Magdalena Zych, head of the research group at the University of Queensland, argues that superposition of states is not only a property of elementary particles, but also of time. Under that concept, the cat in Schrödinger's example would not be alive and dead at the same time, but would be eating and being poisoned at the same time in an endless spiral.

The Soul through Time

We could spend a long time trying to understand the meaning of time and how it relates to other dimensions, but I will try to explain the unexplainable based on what other experts in regressive hypnosis have found, as is the case of José Luis Cabouli, one of my teachers in the field, but mainly from what I myself have found in sessions with my clients.

When I started practicing hypnosis, I used the only technique I knew at the time, the Quantum Healing Hypnosis Technique (QHHT), developed by Dolores Cannon. At that stage, I was able to notice how certain people with physical or psycho-emotional symptoms found relief by returning to the past life in which that discomfort had originated.

To cite a few examples, I saw people with glossophobia (anxiety or fear of public speaking) return to supposed past lives where they had been sentenced or hanged in front of a crowd. For some reason, their body reacted exactly the same as when they were executed. They felt anxiety, fear, shortness of breath, and stiffness in the body, among other ailments. Somehow, their soul remembered having faced a similar situation, causing incomprehensible and uncontrollable reactions.

Other clients suffering from allergies and various skin problems would return to a past reincarnation where they had been burned at the stake—to cite just one of the many explanations I myself have seen—and, for some reason, their soul remembered that event when faced with a similar circumstance of injustice.

I also received people with unexplained pain who did not get clear answers in their medical examinations. Those conditions had no scientific justification, but they felt them and it affected their daily lives. It was no longer a surprise to find out that the root of those symptoms lay in their past lives. It could be that the person had suffered a wound or injury in that same area from a dagger, sword, bullet, or other weapon.

For some reason, the soul remembered those events, which were usually associated with the agony of a previous body. It is the same process that occurs with a childhood trauma. It can cause us, if we face a similar event or experience a similar emotion today, to react just as we did when we were children.

In the same way that a trauma is recorded in our subconscious—whether we remember that event or not—, it can affect us in the future and dictate how we will react to a similar situation. The soul of these clients stored that information and caused them to respond to different situations.

Another thing I noticed with these clients was that, upon visiting the scene of a past life in which the trauma or ailment occurred, the symptom in the current body usually disappeared. How was this possible? It didn't matter how deep their hypnotic trance had been or whether or not they remembered what they had experienced when they came out of that state, the result was always the same.

As time went by, I learned additional techniques, such as Introspective Hypnosis, based on the technique of Colombian hypnotherapist Aurelio Mejía; Life Between Lives, created by American Michael Newton; and finally, Past Life Therapy (PLT), created by Argentinean José Luis Cabouli.

Although I continued to guide my clients in the search for the origin of their ailments, generally located in past lives, obtaining similar results, it was not until I came to know the work of José Luis Cabouli that I understood why they brought to the present these physical and psychological manifestations of a past body.

The reality is that the soul does not understand time. It may be that 3,000 years ago, in a past life in Egypt, you were buried alive, but, to your soul and spirit this has just happened and is still happening. The present, past, and future is only a creation of the human brain to understand time, but the truth is that everything happens now.

What we understand as past lives are, in reality, lives that are happening right now in another timeline. This would be the same as what the prestigious physicist Magdalena Zych says; that everything happens now in an endless spiral. So, the past is not past because it is with us now.

In the example of life in Egypt, where you may have developed claustrophobia before you died, it is more than certain that those same symptoms may present themselves in a subsequent body, causing you to react as you did in that tomb just by being in an elevator or in an enclosed environment.

Why? The answer is simple: The spirit never dies and, for it, life is only one life with experiences in different bodies. If our spirit (soul) did not process some event correctly in some body it had previously, this symptom will follow us from body to body; from reincarnation to reincarnation.

I will share a paragraph from the book *Workers of the Life Eternal*, psychographed by Chico Xavier, where Barceló, a spirit assistant of the group of helpers that was destined to support disincarnated, mentally ill people—who in turn was a teacher when he was reincarnated in the physical plane—explains to André Luiz the importance of understanding that the information stored in our subconscious is not limited to the time of life in the physical body, but goes even further:

> *The subconscious is, in fact, the enlarged vault of our memories, a repository of emotions and desires, impulses and tendencies which are not projected onto the screen of immediate realizations, but which extend well beyond the limited realm of time in which a corporeal body moves. The subconscious represents the stratification of all the struggles resulting in mental and emotional acquisitions after the utilization of many bodies.*

This phenomenon is also known as soul entrapment, in which part of our energy is trapped in the event that was not processed correctly, causing us to relive it over and over again.

Not understanding that time does not exist and that everything happens now is what limits the work of a hypnotist or hypnotherapist in past life regressions, without them even realizing it. What makes all of this even more confusing for practitioners in the field is conducting sessions in linear time (past, present, and future) for a better understanding of our clients, but in turn, having to analyze them and use both past lives and current life memories therapeutically in the present time, in the now; in quantum time.

To better explain this concept, I will use an example of my own invention:

Let's just say that John, who has suffered from chronic back pain for a few years now, decided to schedule an Introspective Hypnosis session with me. John has been to several doctors for tests, but they have not found any physical problem that was triggering this ailment. He has also tried different alternative therapies to deal with this condition, but with no positive results.

For this example, let us assume that John had the following past lives: Egypt in 2589 BC, Rome in 509 BC, France in 1789, two lives in the United States in 1861 and 1889 respectively, and in his current life he lives in Colombia.

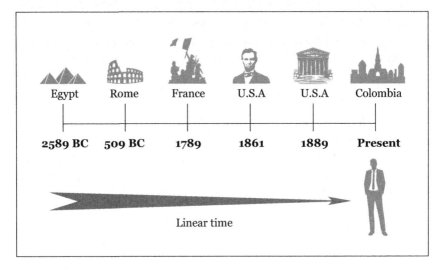

The graph is representing the lives in other bodies in linear time, in a sequence of past and present, so that it is easy to understand.

Let's say that, already in a trance, while searching for the origin of his back pain, John is transported to his past life in France, to the moment when he participates in a battle.

Once there, he begins to describe in detail what is happening around him. He says that many people are dead, that people are fighting with swords. He explains to me that he is afraid because he knows they are at a disadvantage with the enemy and, from one moment to the next, he emits a moan of pain, saying "My back! What a pain!" When I ask him about what is happening, John replies that a sword has been stuck in his back.

I then ask him what he is feeling in his body, the emotions he is experiencing, and what is going on around him—if you notice, my questions are asked in the present tense. John tells me that his body is shutting down, that he is having difficulty breathing and that he is thinking about leaving his children and wife unprotected. We can even add that during the last minutes of his life, he is thinking that this battle is absurd and that he and others are dying for a meaningless cause.

In short, in his last minutes of life, John generated a kind of tunnel vision as he thought about the injustice of the situation and the future of his family. It would be this vision that would not allow him to be aware of all that is happening to him on three levels: physical, emotional, and mental. In other words, his soul did not process the death correctly and this is what will cause part of his energy to be trapped in that experience, and what will cause him back pain in the bodies he will occupy in the future.

As part of the therapeutic work, I help him to become aware of everything that was happening while he was dying and I accompany him until the moment when his soul leaves that body, telling him that, with the death of that body, that experience is over forever and that nothing of what he has experienced will affect him negatively in the future. When he comes out of the hypnotic trance, that back pain has disappeared.

Now, if we think in linear time (past, present, and future), we could assume that, if the pain originated in the life in France and in the present life he lives in Colombia, the pain he brought to the present also had it in the lives that followed after the one in France, that is, the two in the United States.

Well, it is not really that he was born in those lives with that ailment, but that it could have appeared, as it did in his current life, when he was experiencing some emotion similar to the one he experienced while dying in France. Perhaps, when he felt concerned about providing for his family and not leaving them helpless.

So far, we have seen the linear time representation of John's past lives, the way the human brain understands time. Now, we will see how these supposed past lives actually work and affect us.

In this second graph, we can see that the past lives do not occur in a linear sequence, but all happen at the same time. That is why they have been placed around John.

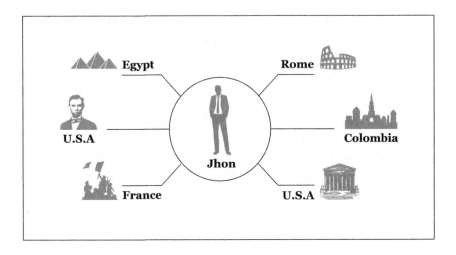

If we understand that past lives are not really past, but simultaneous in an alternate timeline, we can realize that everything that happens in other lives affects John; and, that everything that affects him, affects those lives and those other bodies he has occupied. Everything is connected because we are one soul, one spirit.

Now, going one step further, let's think about the battle and subsequent death in France from that perspective. While I was able to help heal that earlier experience, we could deduce that I also helped heal all the other lives interconnected to his soul and spirit.

If we helped John in a past life, we are helping him in something that is happening now. That's why the back pain he had in his current body disappeared.

In this example, I have explained one of the most confusing concepts for a therapist. When I explain this point in the Introspective Hypnosis courses I teach, I always have to spend extra time on it. It is difficult to question and dismantle an idea that we are taught from birth.

Understanding these concepts will give us the flexibility we need to have while facilitating hypnosis sessions because, in doing so, we will realize that we can apply all the techniques we have learned at all times, regardless of whether it is a recent event, from childhood or from a previous body.

To better reinforce the relationship of the soul and time, I believe it is important to show the reader some sessions that I have facilitated over the years. Most of the client names I will use in this book have been changed to protect their identity. Only a few gave me permission to put their real name. All conversations during the hypnosis trances I will present are true and have been transcribed as they occurred.

Thrown from a Balcony

Sophia came in for an Introspective Hypnosis session to deal with some emotional situations she was going through. When I saw her enter my office, I noticed that she was walking slowly and very carefully, as if she did not have good balance.

Among the physical problems she mentioned during our initial interview was chronic back pain that she had been experiencing for a little over twenty years. That was the reason she had difficulty walking and standing up after sitting for a while. She had visited a doctor on a few occasions, but he had found nothing to justify what she was feeling. However, the pain was still there.

While in trance, Sophia visited a past life in which she was a slave girl of African descent who, along with her mother, worked in the house of a plantation owner. It was through this man that she experienced all kinds of abuse and was exposed to very sad situations. When I asked her to go to the next key scene of that reincarnation, she went to when she was already a young married woman who had been freed from slavery.

Her husband was an alcoholic and constantly abused her. As she told me about her arguments with him and his aggressiveness, I could see the look of terror on her face. When I asked her where she was, she told me she was on a balcony or terrace.

Sophia: "I fell from a balcony," she said with a pained expression on her face.

Antonio: How old are you there?

S: Thirty.

A: How did that happen?

S: Someone pushed me.

A: What's going on while you're being pushed?

S: I am shouting.

A: As you fall?

S: "Yes," she answered while moaning from the pain.

A: What is happening?

S: I hit the ground.

A: And while that is happening, what are your physical reactions? What is happening to your physical body?

At this point, I wanted her to relive that experience so that she could become aware of what was happening to her body. If Sophia had returned to that event, it was because there was something unfinished, something pending that needed to be finished.

S: "It's broken," she answered.

A: And, while your body is broken, what are your emotional reactions at that time?

S: None.

A: And, what are your mental reactions while your body is broken and you feel no emotions?

S: I am going to die. I am going to die.

A: How does this affect you in your life as Sophia? All these feelings, what do they make you do?

S: Feeling pain.

A: And that pain, what does that stop you from doing in your life as Sophia?

S: Walking. It hurts when I walk.

We had found the source of her back pain and walking problems in her current body. Now, I had to help her to close that chapter, to release some of the energy that had been trapped in that event, not having correctly processed the death of her body.

A: "Let's see how this experience begins. I'm going to count from three to one and I want you to go to the moment when you are being pushed.

Notice who's pushing you"—note that the questions I ask are always in the present tense. "Three, two, one. You're already there. What's happening before you're pushed?"

S: "He is my husband!" she said surprised.

A: Why is he pushing you?

S: "He's drunk," he replied while shaking his head from side to side.

A: And what else is going on?

S: He tells me I'm a good-for-nothing.

A: Why is he telling you that?

S: I tried to prepare dinner, but I could not. I am sick.

A: Do you have children?

S: No.

A: What is happening now?

S: "I'm sick," she replied as she began to breathe rapidly, "and he's holding me down."

A: What happens next?

S: He's shaking me.

A: What happens next?

S: He's telling me I'm worthless. He's pushing me! Oh, God!

A: I'm going to count from three to one and you will go back to the instant he is pushing you, but this time allow your body to feel whatever it needs to feel to end this experience forever. Three, two, one. You're already there. What's happening?

S: Oh, God! I am dying.

A: Have you fallen on the floor?

S: Yes.

A: I'm going to count from three to one and when I get to one, I'll touch your forehead and you'll feel the moment when you get hit harder. Three, two, one. Feel that.

S: "Oh, God!" she said, screaming and shaking her head from side to side. "My back is killing me."

A: And, while your back is killing you, how does the spine feel?

S: It hurts!

A: And, while your spine hurts, what do your lungs feel?

S: They are collapsing.

A: And, while that is taking place, what does your heart feel?

S: "It's... it's..."—the pain was so much that she could not finish the description of what she was feeling.

A: And, while that's going on, what is your brain feeling?

S: It's scared!

A: What is the last thought you have in that brain?

S: He killed me!

Up to that moment, I had helped her relive the instant of his death, allowing her to become aware this time of what had happened on a physical, emotional, and mental level; making him feel everything anew and with more intensity.

A: Now, move to the instant you leave your body, understanding that, with the death of that body, this experience is over forever and nothing will affect you.

The session continued for a few more minutes as we evaluated the lessons to be learned in that life and visited others looking for the source of other ailments.

At the end of the experience, I gave her a few minutes to recover, as the experience had been intense and had worked on several of her emotions. When Sophia finally recovered, I saw on her face an expression of amazement and joy at the same time. Her back pain was completely gone.

S: Look! I can get up without pain. I can put on my shoes without any problems. I've had that pain for twenty years and I don't have it anymore.

This case is one of many I have witnessed in which it is clearly shown that the soul knows no time. Sophia had experienced that death many, many years ago, but, to her spirit, it had just happened. That is why she felt the same back discomfort she felt in that body.

This is not to say that Sophia, who was in her early sixties when I facilitated her session, had been born with that ailment in this lifetime. The pain had begun to manifest itself about twenty years ago, when she began to experience the same emotions she had during that event, but this time caused by people from her current reincarnation.

Burning Hands

During the Introspective Hypnosis courses I teach, it is quite common to notice that the emotions, symptoms, and traumas that trainees bring to class manifest in different ways. This happens over the course of the days as I teach different techniques, as I give demonstrations, and as the participants practice on each other.

It is normal that, before I teach them how to perform hypnotic inductions, I perform an induction on them all so that they can experience a trance before understanding how and why it works.

During the live online training I conducted in July 2020, after bringing the participants out of the trance they were in, I could see that Ophelie was not feeling well and was experiencing some discomfort. When I asked her, she told me that she had a headache and felt hot all over her body. Immediately, I knew that she was in an experience from another life and that the symptom she was experiencing was coming from there.

I put her back into trance to relieve her discomfort through a couple of post-hypnotic suggestions, but I also instructed her to contact me after class to talk. I didn't want to tell her in front of everyone what I suspected so that she could feel calm until the end of the learning day.

At the time of the post hypnotic suggestions, it was time for the one-hour lunch break. To my surprise, when I checked my cell phone I found several messages from other participants telling me that Ophelie was not feeling well and asking me to come back and help her.

I noticed Ophelie blushing from the heat she was feeling. She had tears in her eyes and was breathing deeply. So, I proceeded to ask her what she was feeling, while asking her to focus more and more on that.

Antonio: I want you to feel your body. What are you feeling? What emotions are you feeling?

Ophelie: I don't feel any emotion, just a tingling that runs up my feet, past my knees, and into my hands.

A: Let yourself feel that tingle even more. I'm going to count from one to five and we're going to make it even more intense. One. Make it more intense. Two. Feel that tingle. Three. Feel it even more. Four, five. That's good.

I could see the symptom intensifying in her body. Ophelie was crying and having trouble breathing normally.

A: I'm going to count from three to one and you will go to the place where you are feeling that. Three, two, one. You're already there. Like you know, where are you while you're feeling this tingling? Even though you think you're making it up.

Ophelie began to show increased difficulty breathing, as she moved her body from side to side. She was crying, raising her hands to her chest. The symptom was simply unbearable for her.

O: "I don't know where I am. I can only feel my hands," she continued complaining, unable to finish the sentence.

A: What are you wearing? Look at your feet.

O: They look like sandals.

A: Is that male or female?

O: I am a woman.

A: Young or old? Feel the body.

O: Young

A: What are you wearing?

O: A brown skirt.

A: Look at your hands, what's going on with your hands?

O: "I don't feel them anymore," she answered crying and with signs of pain.

A: Look at your feet, what's happening to your feet?

O: I can't move.

A: Are you lying down or sitting?

O: I am standing.

A: And if you knew, why do you think it is that you can't move?

O: It's like an ancient village.

A: What prevents you from being able to move your hands and feet?

O: "There's something heavy," she replied, sobbing, and pointing her head toward her hands, as if she were there again looking at them.

A: Why do you think they put that on your arms and legs? What happened?

O: So that I can't move.

A: I'm going to count from three to one and let's see how this experience begins. Three, two, one. You're already there.

O: I am in nature surrounded by trees. I love trees. I am connected to them.

Suddenly, her voice changed and she sounded very frightened.

O: I can feel them coming.

A: Who are coming?

O: Some people.

A: How do you feel as you find out that these people are coming?

O: I am scared.

A: Move to the moment when these people arrive. Three, two, one. Allow your body to feel everything.

O: I have been caged

A: Why do you think you have been caged?

O: So that I don't do magic.

A: And what magic do you do?

O: I connect with the birds. I connect with the energy of life.

A: And, so far, what has been the most difficult moment while you were being put in the cage?

O: Loneliness.

A: I'm going to count from three to one and you will feel that loneliness more intensely. Three, two, one. You're already there. What are your physical reactions?

O: My stomach hurts.

A: What is happening with your stomach?

O: It burns!

A: What are your emotional reactions as your stomach burns?

O: "I know I'm going to die," she replied, crying inconsolably.

A: What are your mental reactions when you know you are going to die?

O: I have accepted it.

A: And, those feelings, how do they affect your life as Ophelie?

O: I give up.

A: Very good. And, when you give up, what do you stop yourself from doing?

O: Not to be hurt.

A: Go ahead and see what else happens after you are put in the cage. What is happening now?

At that moment, Ophelia began to cry inconsolably, as if giving up and unable to avoid what was going to happen next.

O: Everyone surrounds me. They all hate me and accuse me of being a witch.

A: Move forward a little bit. Is this where that body dies?

O: Yes.

A: Move to the moment when that body begins to die. Three, two, one. You're already there. What's happening?

O: They are burning me! My hands and legs are burning.

We had found the origin of the symptom that Ophelie felt in her present body, the heat all over her body, the hands that she did not feel and the intense tingling in her legs. Everything had been generated in the life of the woman who was burned to death, unjustly accused of being a witch.

Ophelie's soul was trapped in that experience, which seemed to have taken place many years ago, but for her it was just happening. The past was not the past. The past was now present in her body and it was causing her pain.

Her soul had not forgiven those who had burned her unjustly and ignorantly. That was why she kept reliving that moment over and over again. We continued the session for a few more minutes. I helped her to become aware of everything she was experiencing on a physical, emotional, and mental level so that she could close that chapter forever and free her soul from it.

When I asked her what her spirit needed to learn from that life, her answer was: forgiveness. After that online session, Ophelie was able to forgive and rid her soul of that experience forever.

When we brought her out of the trance, she looked exhausted, but the symptoms had completely disappeared. This session had been an excellent example for those attending the course, who could not get over their amazement.

The Innocent Maid

Martha came to my office with a desire to experience a past life regression. During our initial dialogue, she told me about an annoyance she had in her neck for as long as she could remember. The discomfort was so great that it would not allow her to wear anything around her neck.

Immediately, the description of her symptom made me suspect that it was coming from another body, but I did not mention it to her as this could make her nervous and hurt the process.

During the hypnotic regression, I gradually took Martha back in time to a younger age, then to her childhood and from there to the time when she was in her mother's womb, a stage from which we obtained a lot of information and answers. Next, I instructed her to visualize a kind of time tunnel, which she went through as I counted. At the end of this process, Martha was already in another life.

Antonio: Look at your feet and tell me what you are wearing.

Martha: Black shoes with straps, like a girl's shoes.

A: Very good. Now, see what you're wearing.

M: A dress and an apron. And I have some white socks.

A: What color is your skin?

M: White.

A: What color is your hair?

M: Blond.

A: Is the body young or adult, male or female?

M: Young. Female.

A: See if you have any ornaments on your arms or head.

M: I have something on my head. I think it's a hat.

A: What color is it?

M: White.

A: What about your apron?

M: White.

A: Look around you, what do you see?

M: A lot of people. It's like an ancient time, long dresses and hats. It's a very old time.

A: How do you feel there?

M: I am afraid.

A: Why are you afraid?

M: "I don't know," she answered shyly, "but I'm afraid."

A: Keep walking and tell me everything you see around you.

M: It's a square with a lot of people around, as if they were watching something. I'm there walking. I see something made of wood.

A: And, that wooden thing, what does it look like? People are around that wooden thing?

M: Yes. It's like when they are going to sacrifice or hang someone.

Up to this point Martha had no idea what she was seeing, but I had a strong suspicion of what was going to happen and what she was going to experience.

A: Do you see anyone on that wooden thing or not?

M: There are two people. They are two men.

A: Pay attention, what are people saying?

M: "Poor thing, she doesn't deserve that," she replied as she began to cry, as if she was already realizing what was happening.

A: And, how do you feel about seeing that?

M: "Scared," she said, crying deeply as her breath hitched, "I'm so scared!"

A: Are they going to do something to you or is it someone else?

M: "Me," she said surprised and crying.

A: Have you done anything to make them do that to you?

M: No, I haven't done anything!

A: What are they accusing you of?

M: I don't know!

A: Let's find out. We're going to go back to the moment you're caught or charged.

When Martha stepped back as she was being detained, she told me that she was in a large house and that a lady in a black dress was accusing her of something. When I asked her to look that woman in the eyes and tell me if she had seen those eyes in her current life, she tearfully replied that they were those of her sister-in-law, with whom she happened to have had many problems.

The woman had accused her of stealing jewelry from her when in fact she had not. Martha worked as a maid in that house and her name in that life was María and, at that time, she was seventeen years old. María (Martha) told me that, when someone is accused, they are sentenced to hang, and, in this case, the lady was very powerful.

I asked María to travel a little further on. When she did, she began to tell me that a man with his face covered seized her and took her away with her hands tied, informing her that she was going to be hanged.

A: Fast forward to when they are on the wooden structure. What are they going to do there?

M: "They are putting the noose around my neck. I am very afraid. People cry a lot because I am young. They hang me and leave me there alone," she said, crying inconsolably.

A: Move the moment you come out of the body. There is no more suffering. Now that you are out of the body, what do you see below? Are you floating?

M: Yes, I see the people gathered and walking, but I am calm. I feel no pain, no fear.

A: Do you realize that death is an illusion? Now, if we take stock of that life that has ended, what do you think you should have learned from it?

M: To defend myself, to be stronger.

A: And, do you think you passed the test?

M: No.

A: I ask you another question, were you by any chance supposed to learn about forgiveness?

M: Yes.

A: Did you forgive?

M: No.

María had not forgiven those who had unjustly accused and killed her. Moreover, as she was hanged and feeling fear and rage, she could not process the death of that body correctly, without fully feeling that experience on a physical, emotional, and mental level. That is why her soul remained trapped in that event, feeling that death over and over again.

For that reason, in life as Martha, her soul had that symptom in her neck. She felt the rope with which María was hanged.

***

My intention up to this point has been to explain the concept of time from the point of view of the spirit or soul. We have been able to clearly appreciate through these three cases that the soul brings with it traumatic events that occurred in other bodies, manifesting them in the present one.

The reason those events were traumatic is because they were not processed optimally, causing what we know as soul entrapment. Understanding this, it will be easier to understand why a soul can get lost once it dies. We will see different reasons for this, but, in most cases, I have been able to perceive that its entrapment took place during the agony of the body.

LOST SOULS

As I mentioned at the beginning of this book, we understand the soul as a field of conscious energy with its own intelligence that, in spite of being part of a whole, like the divine light, keeps its own individuality and characteristics. Being part of a whole, this energy has access to collective intelligence and experiences and which it uses for its own evolution.

The main motivation of the spirit, which is the soul outside the body, is to progress through the accumulation of experiences in different bodies and dimensions. The planet Earth is only one of the many schools in the universe where we spirits come to learn through emotions.

When the spirit plans its next reincarnation, it structures it meticulously, as if it were a great play tailored to its own evolution. In that staging, it will define the role it will play and the role that others will play in that life and, as in any play, there will be heroes, villains, victims, and aggressors. Contracts will be made with other spirits to interact with them and define the karma—the law of balance in which it will be our turn to feel in equal or greater intensity what we made someone else feel—that must be paid.

In this planning process, the spirit also chooses its parents, through whom it will experience different situations, and chooses the geographical place and time of its birth. In other words, the spirit plans in detail what it will need to live through in order to accumulate experiences and evolve, learning in love or suffering.

Although it is true that everything is programmed in detail and the spirit itself chooses the lessons and events that it will face once in the body, does this mean that its life will be on a kind of autopilot or that its future will be predestined and cannot be altered? No, because both in the spiritual world and once reincarnated, the spirit has free will; that is to say, the power to decide whether it will want to face those lessons or not, or if it prefers to deviate from the marked path.

There are a number of factors that can make that spirit forget what it came to learn or simply close its eyes and decide not to face the obstacles planned before birth. I am referring to the family environment: the culture in which they were born, the religion, the teachings at school, the attachment to the family, the partner, among others.

To give a better idea of what I am trying to explain, I will share again some paragraphs from the book *The Messengers* by André Luiz, where Tobias communicates with him referring to spirits with mediumship gifts that are sent to Earth with a specific task:

> *Many, many spirits are trained here to spread hope and consolation, and to provide instruction and counsel in the various arenas of the planet's evolution. I don't mean just invisible emissaries, however. We also train tightly-knit groups for reincarnation and mediums and instructors leave by the hundreds every year. Those who will be involved in providing spiritual comfort are trained by our messenger center and are sent to the incarnated realms in considerable numbers (...)*

> *You have not yet considered, my dear André, the fact that this preparation in and of itself does not mean they'll be successful. Thousands of qualified messengers leave here, but the ones that actually succeed are rare indeed. Some manage to accomplish their task partially, but most fail completely.*

It must be remembered that this is the description made from the spiritual world.

> *Because we are almost all still to a long history of heinous wrongdoings that have deformed our personalities, few of us succeed. In*

each new life of incarnate endeavor, we believe much more in the demeaning tendencies of our past than in the divine potential of the present, a fact that always has negative implications for the future.

This means that, although we spirits come with a defined learning plan or with specific functions and missions, this does not guarantee a successful outcome. In Tobias' communication, reference is even made to spirits who reincarnate with mediumship gifts, but who, due to life's own demands, deviate from the path or simply decide not to embrace that virtue due to discrimination, fear, or routine.

We are all exposed to the difficulties of this world and to our own free will.

Why Does a Soul Get Lost?

During my training with hypnotherapist José Luis Cabouli, I heard him say something that made a lot of sense to me. I remember he was talking about the process of death and how important it is for a person to be aware of what is happening to their body in order to become aware of their passing when he said, "it is at death that we bring our entire reincarnation into play."

What Cabouli meant by this was that, if the moment of departure was not processed correctly, our soul could become trapped in that experience causing us problems in our next reincarnation and even preventing us from returning to the spirit world. This is one of the forms of soul entrapment known as *post mortem* entrapment.

But why would a soul remain trapped after its body dies? For this question, there is not just one answer. Therefore, I have decided to share my opinion based not only on what I have learned from my teachers but also on what I have been able to verify through my own sessions. For me, a spirit can get lost or trapped both consciously and unconsciously.

Unconscious Entrapment

When we speak of unconscious entrapment, we refer to those cases where the body was not conscious at the time of death and even before it. If the soul has not become aware that the body has died due to the state of confusion in which it finds itself, it may think that it still has a body when in fact it does not. This could occur in the following cases, to mention a few:

- Death by overdose
- Death in coma
- Death under the effects of anesthesia
- Death due to gas or smoke inhalation
- Heart attack
- Tragic accidents
- Homicides

What is common in this type of death is the lack of consciousness of the body at the time of death and that it was instantaneous. When the soul awakens in the other dimension, it is in a state of confusion and bewilderment. In this condition, it is very possible that it does not pay attention to what is happening around it, such as seeing the light or beings of light that come to help it transcend.

When death follows the natural process, the organs begin to fail and the soul begins a process of gradual detachment from the body, often being assisted by other spirits to facilitate it.

There are a number of signs or manifestations in the dying process:

- Weight loss
- Temperature drop
- Change in skin tone
- Change in breathing rhythm
- Hallucinations

I have used the word hallucination because that is how Western medicine describes it, but what actually happens is that the dying person, during the process of detachment, begins to have access to the spiritual dimension. It is not uncommon for them to see people (spirits) in the room or hear voices that we cannot perceive.

If we refer to the cases I mentioned in the section on death, according to the Spiritism doctrine, we will remember that in André Luiz's description we are given to understand the process of detachment as something gradual, where even deceased loved ones can be present and ready to guide us once the soul leaves the body.

Another type of unconscious entrapment occurs when the spirit has not had enough time to process the death. This is the case with instantaneous deaths:

- Tragic accidents

- Heart attack

- Homicides

In these outcomes, the body was conscious but death took place so quickly that the soul did not have time to process what was happening. It is for this reason that it could not experience a gradual detachment either, as explained above, but rather an abrupt and immediate one.

In both types of death, the result is the same: the confusion of the spirit when it finds itself in a new state; in a more subtle one in another dimension.

A Ghost in the House

For me, the best way to explain this concept is with Christian's session, which occurred in 2014. At that time, I had just learned the Quantum Healing Hypnosis Technique and was constantly looking for practice sessions to continue learning and practicing different ways to facilitate hypnosis sessions. So I asked my friend Christian if he would volunteer for such a session. He was attracted to metaphysical topics, so he agreed immediately.

Dolores Cannon's technique is based on past life regressions. At that time, I was not yet aware of the other three techniques that I would later learn that would give me the knowledge about lost souls and soul entrapment. It would take a few years to understand what had actually taken place in that session.

Below is the dialogue from the first past life Christian visited:

Christian: I am inside a house.

Antonio: Look at your feet, what are you wearing?

C: Shoes.

A: Touch your body and tell me if you are male or female.

C: It's me.

A: I want you to describe that house to me from the inside. What is the first thing you see when you enter it?

C: "Wood. There are bleachers," he answered in a slow voice, corresponding to a deep trance. "It is big."

A: Are the steps to enter the house or are they inside?

C: To the left.

A: Tell me about the rooms in that house.

C: High ceilings and large lamps. There are several rooms.

A: Is there anyone else there with you?

C: It is empty. The furniture is covered with cloth.

A: Are they covered because it is not inhabited?

C: Yes.

A: Look for the kitchen and describe to me what you see.

C: It is large and has many windows.

A: Where do you cook?

C: There is an oven.

A: What do you light it with?

C: Firewood.

A: Are you young or old?

C: I don't know.

A: Touch your body, how does it feel?

C: Strong.

A: And what do you do in that house? Is that the place where you live?

C: I don't know.

A: Come out of the house and tell me what you see outside.

C: Countryside. A beautiful landscape.

A: How are they transported?

C: I don't know.

A: Tell me if there is anyone or if you see animals.

C: There is no one.

Supposedly, Christian was visiting a past life in an ancient time, but I could tell he was confused. He did not know who he was, what he was doing there or if that was his home. He saw a wheat field but didn't know by whom or how it was cultivated.

So, we began to look for answers as to how he had come to that empty house and that kind of farm without knowing anything about it.

A: Let's leave that scene. I want you to move in time and space to another important event in that life.

C: There are people.

A: Where are you?

C: In a village. People look at me because I am a stranger.

A: Don't you belong there?

C: I don't know.

A: What are the other people doing?

C: They talk and drink. They wear hats and boots.

A: How did you get there?

C: On foot.

A: What are you doing in that place?

C: I don't know.

A: Do you know how people are transported there?

C: On horseback and in carts.

A: But you arrived on foot, did you have to walk a long way?

C: I don't know.

A: Where do you think your home is?

C: I don't know.

He continued describing the place to me, where there were friendly women smiling at him and men who were annoyed because of it. The women wore strange, flared dresses. He was still dressed the same way, but he mentioned to me that the men were wearing vests. This made me suspect he was in the Old West era, something he would later confirm for me.

I was facilitating that session as an ordinary past life regression. So, trying to find out how he had gotten to that town, I asked him to go back in time. He came to a kind of stable where he was feeding a horse. After asking him a few more questions and leaving that space, we realized that he was back at the same farm where the session had started.

Now, he was in front of the same house, but this time there was a light on. I asked him to come in and start describing each room. He said the same thing about the kitchen, but this time there were people there eating meat and potatoes.

A: Do you know anyone there?

C: No, but they are friendly.

A: Do you think maybe you work for them? They're nothing of yours?

C: I don't know.

A: You can approach them and ask them what you are doing there.

C: "They don't see me," he answered calmly.

A: Try approaching them.

C: I am in front of them, but they don't see me. They are a boy, a girl, and a woman. They are alone.

A: And where will the man of the house be?

C: It's me! But they don't see me.

A: Why do you think they don't see you? Have you tried talking to them?

C: Yes.

A: Can you touch things and move them?

C: No.

At this point, I was almost certain that the man was already on the spiritual plane and that was why he could not be seen or heard.

A: So you feel that it is your home....

C: "I'm there," he interrupted me in distress, "but they can't see me."

The man began to cry desperately, not understanding why his wife and children could not see him. Several times he repeated in anguish "they are there, but they don't see me." I tried to instruct him to go back in time to find out the reason for this, but he was still very confused about what was happening.

Finally, after a few minutes, I was able to calm him down and he was able to travel to another scene from that reincarnation. In it, he was playing with his children.

C: I am playing with them. They are two children.

A: Do you feel older?

C: No, I am young and very strong.

A: Are you in the same house?

C: Yes.

A: Tell me what else is going on.

C: It's a nice day and I play with them. I am their dad.

His wife, who was in the kitchen, greets him and he, very cheerfully, tells me that they can see him now. She had brown hair and wore a long cream-colored dress. Between his descriptions, the man let me know how much he loved her.

We moved once again in time, trying to figure out what had happened. He came to a scene where he was working. He told me he was selling animals and making money at something that looked like a fair.

C: They respect me. I have a black coat.

A: What else is going on?

C: I have a black horse and two guns, one on each side. One is a beautiful shotgun with a silver handle. They respect me a lot here and love me.

A: And, are you working at the moment?

C: I sell animals.

A: See if anything has happened so that your family can't see you.

C: "I am being followed," he said suddenly.

A: Who is following you?

C: They are men on horseback. It is daytime.

A: What else is going on?

C: They follow me, but my horse is faster. They want the money. I get home in a hurry.

A: They want the money, then.

C: "Yes, they have taken my wife. They grab her by the hair," he says, crying and having difficulty swallowing saliva. "My children are under a secret table and they can't see them. There are six of them and they want to kill my wife. They shoot her, but I get in and they can't see me anymore!"

The man had realized that he had been killed while trying to defend his wife and, since he had become a spirit, they could no longer see him. Because it happened so quickly and dramatically, he was unaware of the death of that body. That is why, when we started the session, he was in an empty house with the furniture covered. It was more than certain that, after his death, his wife and children had moved out.

As I have already mentioned, at the time I facilitated that session for Christian, I did not yet have the knowledge about lost souls. At that time, I did not realize that what appeared to be Christian's past life was actually the past life of the spirit attached to him, who, once Christian's body was in trance, was able to communicate with me. Perhaps he himself did not know that he was manifesting through a body that was not his own.

I was able to come to that conclusion when I saw that Christian's spirit did not know who he was in that past life, nor his name or other details that, while being in a trance, are easier to access.

Several months later, after learning other techniques, I invited Christian to another hypnosis session without telling him about my suspicions because I did not want to scare him. The truth is that, every time we agreed on the day and time, something always happened that prevented him from coming. This indicated to me that the spirit that was still attached to me already knew that I had noticed and preferred to avoid the meeting, putting all kinds of obstacles in Christian's way.

Moreover, while transcribing his session for this book, I decided to call him and explain my suspicions. So, we arranged to meet a couple of days later, but once again, the meeting did not materialize.

The Firefighter with Amnesia

In 2016, Liliana contacted me by phone to schedule an Introspective Hypnosis session. She did not know who I was, or what kind of techniques I used. She had stumbled upon me on the Internet while searching for someone who practiced hypnosis in Spanish in Charlotte, North Carolina, the city where I reside.

During our initial interview, Liliana told me that sometimes she felt like she was suffocating and the thought of dying came to her mind. She told me that she was afraid that one day her husband would return and find her lifeless. She also told me that she had visited some doctors, but they had not found any cause for this symptom. She had even felt the same thing when she was hooked up to a hospital monitoring system when one of her children was born, and the doctors told her that the monitors did not show that she was suffocating.

In her session, we found two spirits: the first was that of a young woman, who was provoking that symptom; and the second was that of a firefighter, who appeared while I was using the role change technique in one of the memories she visited while in trance.

After going into trance, one of the first issues I faced with Liliana was the origin of the anger she felt towards her father.

Antonio: I am going to count from three to one and you will go to the moment when that rancor starts. Three, two, one. You are already there. What is happening?

Liliana: I am with my dad.

A: So, what's going on?

L: He is angry. I made him angry.

A: What did you do?

L: "I did not obey him," she said in a slow, soft voice, indicating a deep trance.

A: How old are you there?

L: Seven.

A: And what does he do?

L: He is sitting down. He's correcting me, hitting me on the hand.

When someone else is involved in a sad memory of my client, I employ the technique of role reversal, whereby I begin a dialogue with the absent person. Usually, this communication is mental, although, depending on the level of trance, it can also occur on a spiritual scale.

A: I'm going to count from three to one. When I get to one, you're going to let your dad talk to me. Three, two, one. Jesús, good evening. Are you Liliana's father?

L: No.

A: Aren't you Liliana's father?

L: No.

A: Are you Jesús?

L: No.

A: Who are you then?

L: I don't know.

A: Don't you know who you are?

L: No.

A: Let's see, I'm a little confused. We are in a memory in which Liliana is with her father. Are you part of that memory or are you somewhere else?

L: I am somewhere else.

A: Oh, I get it, did you by any chance get attached to it?

Lost Soul: No.

A: Where are you then?

LS: I am here.

A: In this room?

LS: Yes.

A: So, what are you doing here? Are you going to help us?

LS: I don't know.

A: Do you need help?

LS: Yes.

A: Can I ask you a question, how did you find us? If you are not attached to it, how did you find us?

LS: Here I am.

A: I know you are here, but I want to know how you found me. Do you know who I am?

LS: No.

A: Do you know who Liliana is?

LS: No.

A: And just like that you showed up?

LS: I don't know.

Definitely, I was talking to a spirit that saw Liliana in a trance and took the opportunity to communicate. The curious thing is that it was not attached to her but was passing through the same physical space in which we were.

The spirit did not remember several facts of its life. This kind of amnesia is quite common. I myself have encountered many times spirits who did not even remember how their body died. The main thing was that the spirit was lost, confused, and needed help.

A: When you had a body, were you a man or a woman?

LS: Male.

A: How did your body die?

LS: In an accident.

A: What type of accident?

LS: Burned.

A: Do you know what year it was, before or after 1900?

LS: 1900.

A: And where were you when you were burned to death?

LS: I am a firefighter.

His response in the present tense led me to conclude that he still thought he was a firefighter. The strange thing is that we had already discussed his passing, but, as his spirit had not gone into the light, he still retained the ego, i.e., his identity, personality, habits, and beliefs.

A: What country were you from?

LS: From here.

A: You were American?

LS: I don't know.

A: Do you know what your squad, group, or bomb squad was called?

LS: "Red Cross," he answered as if hesitating.

A: And what was your name?

LS: Mario.

A: Do you remember your last name?

LS: Mario.

A: That's your first name, but your last name?

LS: I don't know.

A: When your body burned to death, were you young or old?

LS: Young.

A: Mario, could it be that some of what you felt when you died was transmitted to Liliana?

LS: No.

This confirmed that Mario's spirit was not attached to my client's energy field.

A: Then you definitely have nothing to do with her.

LS: No.

A: So why haven't you gone to the light? What is it that keeps you from going towards it?

LS: I see no light.

A: Generally, when one does not see the light, it is because one has not forgiven something or because one has something unfinished. Was there something unfinished in your life?

LS: No.

A: Children, wife?

LS: No.

A: Did you hurt someone, or did someone hurt you?

LS: No.

A: In other words, your death was an accident.

LS: Yes.

A: And, so, you hung around here looking for what, brother?

LS: Helping.

This answer further confirmed his disorientation, as he thought he was still doing what he was doing before he passed away.

A: So, you think you are still putting out fires, that you are still helping people? What happened is that your body died, but you are a spirit and eternal. Do you understand me?

LS: No

A: So, let me explain. We are spirits and we reincarnate in a physical body on this planet. In your last life, you were a firefighter, but that physical body, which in the long run is just like a suit, no longer exists. So, now you are a spirit again. Do you realize that?

LS: Yes.

A: Without a physical body, it is difficult for you to put out fires because you need hands and legs to be able to carry the hose and pour water. Do you understand?

LS: Yes.

A: You can't do that now.

LS: No.

A: I know you intend to help and that's fine with me, but you don't have a physical body. Do you realize that?

LS: Yes.

A: So, waiting here is pointless. You have to go into the light, and I can help you.

LS: Yes.

So, I proceeded to ask for help from our spiritual brothers, my guide, his spiritual guide, and the rescue team from the light to come for him.

A: Now, I want you to tell me if you see any light or entity coming to guide you.

LS: A young man.

A: And, how does that young man look, brother?

LS: Happy.

A: Does he inspire confidence in you?

LS: Yes.

A: So, are you ready to continue on your path to the light?

LS: Yes.

That day, Mario's spirit departed to the other plane assisted by a being of light. Later, we will revisit Liliana's session to detail the origin of her asphyxia.

As we have been able to appreciate, as in the case of the spirit of the cowboy attached to Christian, many times the spirits do not realize that their physical body has died and continue among us, as if their life goes on, although full of confusion and disengagement. A characteristic in them is the amnesia to which they are exposed, forgetting certain details of their last reincarnation.

A rather interesting and moving session in which a lost soul was found is one facilitated by José Luis Cabouli at the Entrapments and Soul Retrieval workshop, which took place in Mexico in 2019.

During the brief interview Cabouli had with the volunteer beforehand, she mentioned the sadness she felt for the death of her father, which had occurred some years ago. When the Argentine hypnotherapist asked how he had died, she replied that it was due to a fulminant heart attack.

Once the session began, the young woman immediately visited the moment of her parent's passing. "My dad is here!" she exclaimed in tears. Cabouli, sensing what was happening to her father's soul, asked her to ask him if he knew what had happened to his body. She replied that he did not know, while crying.

José Luis Cabouli asked her to explain to his father that he had just suffered a heart attack that had led to his death. After all this time of confusion, his daughter was giving him the news. Then, through the young girl, he told the spirit to look for a being of light or a light around him. The father replied that he saw nothing of the sort. The hypnotherapist, in front of all the attendees, began to pray for him, asking God, in his infinite mercy, to send his angels to pick him up.

The father finally saw the light and his daughter informed him that it was time to leave, but he replied, "I cannot go and leave your mother alone, otherwise who will take care of her?" On Cabouli's instructions, the young girl tearfully asked her father not to worry, that she would take care of her, and told him to go in peace. The two said goodbye. Meanwhile, the audience wept at such a scene.

After seeing his work in that workshop, I enrolled in the Past Life Therapy course he taught in Spain a year later. Among the many things I learned from José Luis that time, there was something he said that stuck with me forever:

When a person is going to die, you have to help them to be aware of what is happening to their body and what is going to happen.

Some people prefer to hide the fact that they are dying from their family members while they are lying in a hospital bed. Some ask the doctor not to give them the news of what is going to happen to them. Others even prefer to keep them asleep (unconscious) in order to avoid their suffering.

We must remember that when we do not process correctly what is happening on a physical, emotional, and mental level during the agony, it is very likely that our soul will end up trapped. Most likely, when that spirit awakens in the other dimension, it will not understand what is happening and will not realize that its body has died.

Conscious Entrapment

We speak of conscious entrapment when the soul knows that its body has died but decides to stay in the physical plane for various reasons. The reasons they may have for remaining here are varied, but I can mention a few that I have come across during the sessions I have conducted:

- Parents who remain watching over their children, because they believe that, by going to the spiritual plane, they would be leaving their children unprotected and need to stay to take care of them. It may also be the case that the parent is overprotective and wants to make sure that their first-born child makes good decisions.

- Couples who wish to continue caring for their loved one. It may be the case of those who want to wait until the partner dies to leave the physical plane together or, perhaps, want to ensure that their partner does not establish a relationship with another partner. It is also often the case of those who feel that they have left their partner in a bad financial situation and helpless.

- Grandparents who stay to watch their grandchildren grow up.

- Friends with whom we shared moments and experiences, and who wish to stay with us.

- Family members who wish to give a message.

- Those who have unfinished business and think that they could not complete their projects or business. Normally, they are people who are very attached to material things and do not accept that they will no longer be able to enjoy them.

The list could be endless, but I want you to get an idea of the varied reasons spirits may have for staying with us and not traveling to the other plane. These reasons may not make sense to us because we think that in the spiritual dimension where they are, they should have a better understanding, but let's remember that, by not going to the light, the spirit keeps its ego, personality, beliefs, habits, and addictions, among other characteristics. In other words, it is basically the same person, but without a body.

The Girl in the Hole

María Magdalena came to my office because she was suffering from a series of unexplained symptoms, such as headaches, dizziness, and vomiting. In addition to these, she had all the physical signs of being pregnant without actually being pregnant.

In order for you to process your session in the best way and differentiate what we encountered that day, I will divide it into two parts.

Already in trance, María Magdalena visited a couple of sad memories from this life, which we worked on with different techniques, ending with forgiveness therapy. As we let her soul and subconscious guide us to other events, we came to a supposed past life in which she was a child in the desert.

Antonio: There where you are, what do you see?

María Magdalena: I don't see anything. It's like a dark hole.

A: You can touch your body and tell me if it feels young or old.

MM: A baby.

A: What is that baby wearing?

MM: She is a little, dark-skinned girl, with Indian features.

A: Where do you see that girl? You can also pay attention to the sounds around you.

MM: I see myself in the desert.

A: And you are that little girl?

MM: Yes.

A: Do you know how old you are more or less?

MM: Seven years.

A: What do they call you there?

MM: I don't know.

A: Walk through the desert sand and see what you are wearing on your feet.

MM: I am barefoot.

A: What are you wearing?

MM: I have a pink dress.

We already knew who she was and where she was. I continued to ask her questions to decipher the story of that past life. She told me that there was a small lake and that she was alone, but there was a man nearby that she did not know. He was dark-skinned and wore a white shirt, black pants and a cloth tied around his head. Near the lake, there were a few empty houses and some camels.

A: How do you feel you got there?

MM: I don't know.

A: Let's move away from that scene. I want you to back up to the moment when you figure out how you get there. Three, two, one. You're already there. What's going on?

MM: I see sand and a row of camels. Her dad is carrying a row of camels.

Here, for some reason, María Magdalena began to speak in the third person, disconnecting herself from the girl. Because of what happened in the previous dialogue, she wanted to find out if the spirit of the girl was attached to her.

A: Let me ask you a question, are you María Magdalena in a past life or are you with María Magdalena?

Lost Soul: "I am with María Magdalena," she answered softly.

A: I get it. When your body had life, what did they call you?

LS: I don't know.

A: Do you know why you have attached to her?

LS: Because she is a brunette and loves her daddy very much.

A: Is that why you have attached to her?

LS: Yes, because I also love my dad very much.

This was an essential piece of information to understand the situation.

A: How did your body die?

LS: "I fell into a dark hole," she said, her voice cracking, as if she was about to cry.

That was the scene she initially described when we came to this past life, which we now knew did not belong to María Magdalena but to the spirit of the girl attached to her.

A: Did you fall by chance?

LS: Yes, Dad couldn't save me.

A: So, I ask you a question, is there anything that you have caused voluntarily or involuntarily to María Magdalena?

LS: The headache. When I fell, my head hurt.

A: And that's what she's feeling?

LS: Yes.

A: What other symptom are you causing?

LS: Dizziness and vomiting.

A: How long have you been with María Magdalena?

LS: Since she was a baby.

A: And where did you find her?

LS: I don't know.

A: Do you know that you are attached to a body that is not yours?

LS: Yes.

A: Do you know how long ago or so your body died?

LS: Yes, in 1950.

A: And, have you ever wondered where your dad is?

LS: I don't know.

A: Because, when you die, you have the choice of going to the light or staying in this plane. Did you stay looking for your father?

LS: Yes.

Again, the spirit of the girl was giving me clues to the outcome of this story.

A: And, have you ever thought that your dad ended his life in his body and is also looking for you?

LS: No.

A: Do you want me to help you look for it?

LS: Yes.

A: All right, then, I want you to go, but come back. Don't stay. I'm going to ask my guide and María Magdalena's guide, the archangel Michael and the archangel Gabriel to show you the way to the light, where your daddy is. Go with them, go to the light and come back. Let me know when you are in the light, can you see them?

LS: Yes, I see light.

A: Can you see the guides?

LS: "I see Jesus," she sighed, "only Jesus."

A: Then, see if your father is close to Jesus.

LS: "He's not there," she said in a voice of sadness and frustration.

A: Ask Jesus if he knows where he is.

LS: "Where is Daddy," she asked aloud. "He says he's María Magdalena's daddy!"

A: He says he is María Magdalena's father?

LS: "Yes!" she answered with a disconsolate cry.

A: I understand. Let me explain, your father passed away and reincarnated as María Magdalena's father, do you understand?

LS: Yes.

A: So, it means he's in good hands because you know she loves him very much, right?

LS: Yes.

This is how we discovered the origin of María Magdalena's symptoms and the reason why the girl's spirit had attached itself to her energy field. Somehow, deep down, she knew it was her father's spirit and decided to follow him regardless of the fact that he was now in another body.

As we could notice in the initial dialogue, in the first scenes of that past life, she was already a lost soul searching for her father. The girl had told me about a man I did not know who was near the small lake in the desert. Would this be her father?

It seems that in the confusion of her death, her spirit did not decide not to go towards the light, but preferred to look for her loved one. Her soul got lost and decided to attach to the vibratory field of María Magdalena.

Imaginary Pregnancy

Once we helped the girl's spirit to go to the spiritual plane, I continued working with María Magdalena. So, she went to another past life—this time it was one of her own—where she was a young girl named Mali.

In one of the scenes of that reincarnation, Mali told me how her mother had given birth to a dead baby. She described what looked like guts on the bed and her sad mother, who then also passed away.

When I asked her to fast forward to the next scene, she came to her wedding day, where she related that everyone was dressed in white, but after a while she could no longer see anything. After this, she told me that she was pregnant and that her belly was very large, a feature that was frowned upon in her culture. When it was time to give birth, the baby was stillborn too.

Then Mali traveled to the last moment of her life, when she was already an old woman. She told me in anguish that there was a child with an ugly expression on his face, who seemed to be evil. I asked her to look into his eyes and tell me if those eyes were or would be in the life of María Magdalena. She answered me "yes", but she did not know who it was. After a few more questions, she told me, "Yes, it is. It is inside her." This would be the key to understand why María Magdalena felt this imaginary pregnancy.

I asked her to go to the phase where she was coming out of her body, but she told me that it was difficult because that child was looking at her ugly. Once Mali's spirit went to the light, I asked to talk to the energy that was with María Magdalena—although Mali's spirit and María Magdalena are the same, they have different bodies and therefore different energy.

Antonio: Brother, you can express yourself now.

Lost Soul: "Yes," he said to me in a mocking voice.

A: Have you been with María for a long time or a short time?

LS: "A long time," he replied with a smile.

A: And who are you?

LS: I am bad.

A: I don't want you to give me a qualifying adjective. I want you to give me your name.

LS: I'm not going to tell you.

A: I think I know your secret.

LS: You don't know.

A: You were Mali's son?

LS: No.

A: Who are you, then?

LS: I am bad.

A: You know that I am here to help you and María Magdalena, right?

LS: Yes.

A: What have you caused María Magdalena, either voluntarily or involuntarily?

LS: Her stomach.

A: Why are you doing that to her? Why are you attached to her?

LS: Because I was a baby who wanted to be born, but I was stillborn.

A: Are you the stillborn baby from Mali?

LS: No, from her mother. My mom died because of me because I was born dead.

A: We all choose when we are born and when we die. Do you think it could be that your mother chose when to leave?

LS: No.

A: Supposing what you say is true, what do you gain by attaching yourself to the body of María Magdalena, who was your sister, Mali?

LS: "Because I want to be born," he replied with a gesture of frustration.

A: You want to be born, but have you realized it's not the right way? First, you have to go to the light, evaluate your short life, plan with your guides, and come back.

LS: But I feel alive here.

A: But it is an illusion.

LS: "No, I am alive inside it," he said very frustrated.

A: See how much confusion there is that María Magdalena thinks you are a gas.

LS: No, she feels something. Her husband has felt me too because I always move at night when she is resting. She gets scared because she doesn't know what it is.

A: So, you think that because you make her belly move, you are going to be born.

LS: Yes.

A: And since how long ago have you been trying?

LS: Very.

A: And why haven't you been born yet? The gestation period is nine months, how long have you been trying?

LS: Four years.

A: Imagine that! That means you can't be a fetus because otherwise you would have been born already.

LS: Yes.

A: It's a confusion. I would also be confused under those circumstances.

Thus, continued my conversation with the spirit of the baby, trying to make him realize that he felt alive because the spirit never dies, but not because he was a baby in María Magdalena's womb waiting to be born.

A: Your mom must be looking for you.

LS: I don't want to go with my mom. I want to be with María Magdalena because she wants another baby.

At this point, I paused, asking the lost soul to wait for me, as I turned to ask María Magdalena's husband, who was present at the session, if it was true that they wanted to have another child. He replied that they did.

To get María Magdalena's version, I put the spirit on hold while I talked to her.

A: María Magdalena, have you heard that we have a spiritual brother who was your little brother in a past life?

María Magdalena: Yes.

A: That energy that moves your belly, have you felt it?

MM: Yes.

A: He tells me he is there because he wants to be born and he wants you to be his mother. What do you think?

MM: "But I want a girl," she said with a frown.

A: Ah, maybe he's been a boy before, but he's a spirit. Would you agree to give him the chance to be born from your womb?

MM: Yes.

A: Could you give him the chance your mom couldn't give him?

MM: Yes, I want him to be born and happy.

So María Magdalena and the baby's spirit agreed to give each other a chance. He apologized for the symptoms he had caused her, gathered his energy, and departed into the light.

The interesting thing about this session was that, while communicating with the spirit of the child, I had to change the batteries twice in the microphone I was using to record the session because it seemed that the spirit's energy was consuming them quickly.

María Magdalena's husband, who was present during the entire meeting, could not believe what he had witnessed.

The Obsessive Spirits

Here I am referring to those spirits whose intention is to attach to our vibratory field (aura) with the sole purpose of causing us problems. There are times, even, that I have found some that are not attached, but still complicate our life.

While we could say that, in a way, they are lost; the truth is that they are lost because of their poor vision of spirituality and ignorance of what it means to reincarnate in this school called planet Earth.

We are talking about:

- Enemies seeking revenge. It can occur in case of debts, homicides, and infidelities, among others.
- Spirits that put themselves at the service of people who perform black magic or witchcraft rituals, even if they have nothing personal against the victim.
- Opportunistic spirits.
- Spirits that identify with our habits and addictions.

These are just a few examples that I have encountered in sessions.

Later on, we will talk about people who are prone to having attached spirits or parasites, as they are also called.

***

As we have seen in this chapter, there are several reasons why a soul can get lost or attach itself to a person's energetic field. No matter if the intentions are good, the result will always be the same: the person will end up affected by the spirit's energy as it will transmit its residual emotions, fears, habits, and even physical pains related to the way their body died.

This is the origin of many of the symptoms that we experience and that have no logical explanation.

There is much psychographed literature provided by beings of light, describing the space between the earthly crust, or physical plane, and the light, which is the highest dimension. Apparently, there is an intermediate zone referred to as the purgatorial zone, which is inhabited by lost and tormented souls who find themselves prey to hells of horror created by themselves in their passionate ravings.

The spirit of André Luiz has provided a detailed description of this space in his various texts. This information has been corroborated to some extent through hypnosis sessions.

SPIRITS IN OUR VIBRATORY FIELD

There are many contradictions when explaining the influence that lost souls can have on human beings. Some call it spirit attachment and call these spirits parasites. There are others who call it possession, referring to a total takeover of the person's body, displacing the soul that originally inhabited it.

The truth is that trying to expose this from a scientific point of view is practically impossible because there is no way to demonstrate what happens when an energy (lost soul) influences a person's body. But let us go by parts. First, let us talk about these concepts in a gradual way in order to reach a better understanding.

The Aura

In parapsychology, the aura is known as the vibratory field around the person. This can be of different colors that are constantly changing, depending on our physical, mental, and emotional health, and the activities we are doing at the moment.

The aura is energy, frequency, and vibration. We could also describe the aura as that part that sends signals to the universe with information about ourselves, attracting certain specific energies. It is believed that the aura, which is not visible to most people, also fulfills other functions, such as filtering harmful energies in all their forms and operating as an antenna or bridge of connection with nourishing energies.

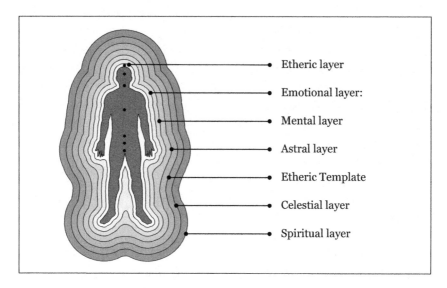

The aura has seven layers that contain the map of our physical body, from our emotions and level of sensibility to our level of evolution:

- **Etheric layer:** it is the closest to our physical body and is connected to our root chakra (energy center).
- **Emotional layer:** contains our emotions, feelings, and sensibility.
- **Mental layer:** comprises our mental processes, such as discipline and judgment.
- **Astral layer:** acts as a bridge connecting low vibrations of the physical plane with the high vibrations of the spiritual plane.
- **Etheric Template:** associated with the aspects of the physical body and is connected to the fifth chakra (throat). This layer contains the plane/template of everything that exists on the physical plane.
- **Celestial layer:** it is the origin of our spiritual connection and contains the template for all the other layers. This layer is also known as the morphic field, given by the British writer Rupert Sheldrake, referring to the fields of structures and patterns.
- **Spiritual layer:** it is the one that protects all the other layers.

As I indicated above, the aura has a unique frequency that identifies us in the universe and behaves like the IP address of a computer connected to the Internet. It is through it that it becomes possible to find each other on a spiritual and energetic level. In this way, our loved ones and enemies who seek us from the subtle dimension come to us to attach themselves to our energetic field or simply to give us a message.

Unlike the chakras, which are spirals of energy that go from the outside in, the aura is energy that the body emits outward from the cells in the form of heat, electromagnetic frequency, or bioplasma.

There are several people who claim to be able to see the aura and, according to a group of professors from the University of Granada, they would actually have synesthesia, which is a neuropsychological alteration characterized by the mixing of the senses.

Ego and Spiritual Consciousness

As we explained at the beginning of this book, the word ego comes from the Latin 'yo' and is used to refer to the consciousness of the individual, causing the person to recognize his or her own identity.

When a spirit begins the process of reincarnation, it also begins a process of integration into the body of the baby (fetus) that it will occupy; from connecting with the brain and neurotransmitters, to connecting with the emotional system of that body.

In this primary stage, which takes months, the spirit does not remain in the body during the nine months of gestation but enters and leaves the womb while making this connection and continues to visit the spiritual world until the day of birth.

The spirit, which has an eternal identity and a name in the spiritual world, will, little by little, be coupled to that identity and ego of the body it will occupy. The combination of the spiritual ego with that of the body it will inhabit will result in a new identity that will bear the name given to us by our parents.

The books *Destiny of Souls* and *Life Between Lives*, by the American hypnotherapist Michael Newton, confirm the characteristics of this system, after thousands of hypnosis sessions with his patients. This is something that I have also been able to verify through the sessions that I facilitated once I was certified in Newton's technique.

One of the greatest challenges for the reincarnated spirit is to adjust to and control the character, emotions, and instincts of the new body in which it will be residing.

Regression to the Mother's Womb

To give a better idea of what happens in the womb as the spirit integrates into the fetal body, I will present an excerpt from the womb regression of Sabrina, who took my Introspective Hypnosis course in 2018.

In that time, I could tell that she went into deep trance very easily. That is why, during my certification with the Newton Institute, I asked her if she would like to volunteer for a session using the Life Between Lives technique, which contains womb regression as a natural part of the procedure.

Antonio: Do you have any feelings or impressions about the body you are going to occupy?

Sabrina: I feel it vibrating.

A: Do you know what is causing it to vibrate?

S: I'm getting used to it.

A: Is it easy to fit into this body?

S: Yes.

A: How does this body compare to others you have inhabited before?

S: It is fragile, it can break and hurt. It can also perceive.

A: How so?

S: It is sensitive.

A: What are your impressions of the last few months that you have been working with the body?

S: "I just got in," she said, referring to becoming fully joined together.

A: How many months of gestation has that body been through?

S: Eight months.

A: And in what months did you enter the body?

S: At eight, but from there I left again and returned at nine months.

A: And, when you go out, where do you go?

S: I go back to my spiritual group, but I go in and out.

A: What is the main characteristic of this body that you are going to occupy?

S: It is very emotional.

A: What have you learned about the emotional system of this body?

S: Neurotransmitters are essential because they play an important role in the body. People know about them scientifically and they have to understand why emotions are so difficult to understand. Neurotransmitters are the energetic connection to the human mind. If they could be manipulated, emotions would not be so complicated to control, but we are not taught this when we go to Earth and are children. Our parents don't know, unless they are doctors or scientists. Neurotransmitters create waves of energy. Human beings are made of that, they are made of a lot of energy. I can see the energy, I can feel it in my hands.

That day, Sabrina gave much more information about the stage of union of the spirit to the human body. What I most appreciated from our dialogue is the complexity of this process.

PARASITIC SPIRITS

Fearing that this term may be, to some extent, offensive to describe a lost soul attached to a person's vibratory field, I decided to use it as a reference to what it does or causes. Let me explain further. The word parasite comes from the Latin word *parasitus* and refers to an organism that lives at the expense of another species, weakening it without causing its death.

In a way, a lost soul who decides to attach itself to the aura of a human being, whether with good intentions or not, is basically doing the same thing: living off their energy, exhausting them, and causing them all kinds of problems.

It is not uncommon for a person with a parasitic spirit to be physically and emotionally tired constantly. We can give the example of a tick that attaches itself to our skin. It does not control us, nor does it displace us to take over our body. But it lives off our blood, weakening us and, in turn, transmitting what we know as Lyme disease, which can cause symptoms such as fever, fatigue, headache, and muscle aches. That is exactly what a parasitic spirit causes when it attaches itself to our aura: fatigue, weakness, and that we experience the symptoms they had when they still had a body.

In the book *Missionaries of the Light*, dictated by the spirit of André Luiz to the medium Chico Xavier, this action is called 'vampirism'. In the same text, Alejandro, a guiding spirit who explained this phenomenon to André Luiz, says the following:

> *You are not aware that in the realm of earthy diseases each microbe species has its preferred environment. The pneumococcus normally lodges in the lungs; Eberth's bacillus is found in the intestines where it produces typhoid fever; the Klebs-Loeffer bacillus settles in the mucous membranes, where it causes diphtheria. (...) But do you think that such microscopic formations are restricted only to the transitory flesh? Don't you know that the macrocosm is full of surprises in varied forms? In the infinitesimal field, the findings follow the same surprising order. André, my fried, psychic illnesses are much more deplorable. The pathogenesis of the soul manifest in many different heartrending ways: anger, intemperance, sexual dissipation and varying degrees of degradations produce inferior creations that deeply affect one's inner life. A sick body almost always indicated a diseased mind.*

What this paragraph is trying to explain to us is that, for the diseases of the soul, before the affliction, there is the environment and the actions that produce effects. This means that, for a parasitic spirit to attach itself to our vibratory field, there must be a favorable space: anger, disappointment, hatred, or vices.

Now, we must understand that a lost soul, not having gone to the light—or heaven, whatever you want to call it—has not yet shed that ego it adopted when it initially incarnated in the body it had. That is to say, the lost soul will have the same personality, beliefs, prejudices, addictions, fears, and phobias, but what is even more worrying, is that they can also keep everything they experienced during the agony of their body, especially the physical pain. All these characteristics will end up being transmitted by the parasitic spirit to its victim.

There may also be circumstances in which a lost soul exerts influence on certain events and happenings. This can be verified in the answers given by the spirits in *The Spirits' Book*, by the French writer Allan Kardec:

Do *spirits* exert *influence over the events of life?*

- Certainly, because they counsel you.

Do they exert this influence in any other way besides the thoughts they suggest? Do they act directly in the outcome of things?

- Yes, but they never act outside natural laws.

The Town on Fire

This time we will return to the session of Liliana, a young woman who came to me in desperation looking for an urgent hypnosis session. I remember her telling me: "I feel like I'm suffocating and I'm afraid that one day my husband will come home and find me dead."

As I mentioned before, during the interview we had, she told me that this was something that happened frequently and that it had been getting worse. Even during the delivery of one of her children, she felt like she was suffocating, but the doctors told her husband that the monitors did not indicate that and that it was probably an emotional symptom.

It should be noted that, most of the time, a lost and attached soul will not let us know that it is there because it has not realized that its body has died or because it has the misconception that we want to force it out and prefers to go unnoticed. Later we will see ways to detect them during a session, paying attention to every word and expression they say during our client's trance state.

Already in a trance, I asked Liliana to go to a sad memory, one that had caused her some discomfort. When I counted from five to one, she immediately went to one in which she and her mother were working at a street stand selling Mexican food. As I asked her questions to get a detailed description of that scene, she started coughing as if she was choking.

Liliana: "I'm choking," she exclaimed while making sounds with her throat.

Antonio: There with your mother?

L: Yes.

A: And why are you choking? Look at the scene from the outside so you can breathe calmly. Why are you choking?

L: I am eating.

A: Do you choke while eating?

L: Yes.

A: Does that always happen to you?

L: Yes.

A: It doesn't matter what you eat?

L: No

She had been experiencing this symptom since her adolescence and, while it is true that we could assume that it originated in this memory, what we should really do is not take anything for granted and ask our clients to look for the first time they had this symptom.

A: Now, I am going to count from three to one and ask your subconscious to take you to another time when you have felt that suffocation. You are a spirit and you can travel in time and space. Search in this or other lifetimes. Go to the root. Three, two, one. You are already there.

L: I am in the field.

A: There, where you are, I want you to look at your feet and tell me what you are wearing.

L: Nothing.

A: Touch your body and tell me what you are wearing.

L: A brown dress.

A: Are you young or old?

L: Young.

A: What is the name of this place you are in?

L: I don't know.

A: What color is your hair?

L: Black.

A: Do you wear anything on your head?

L: A hat.

A: And what is your name?

L: I don't know.

A: What else do you see in the field you are in?

L: Horses. There are many horses.

A: Are they yours?

L: No. They are running.

A: So, what are you doing in that place?

L: I am scared.

A: Why?

L: Because they are running.

I continued to ask her questions about the horses, and she told me that they ran because they were afraid and that she was afraid of them. Liliana, that is, who that woman was in that life, told me that she did not know why they felt that way.

A: Do you live around there?

L: No.

A: And how did you get there?

L: I am standing.

A: Fast forward in time until something happens. This is the origin of your asphyxia, what happens?

L: There are dry trees and lots of air. People come running.

A: What else is going on?

L: They are afraid.

A: Just like horses?

L: "Yes, they don't see me," she said quizzically.

A: And you're standing in front of them?

L: Yes.

A: And they don't see you because they run by or what?

L: "I don't know. They don't see me," she repeated.

A: What else is going on?

L: There is fire.

A: Can you smell it?

L: No, I see it. It's burning.

A: The field?

L: No, the houses.

A: Can you feel the heat?

L: No, I see it. It's my house that's burning.

A: Is that the only one burning or are there more?

L: There is more.

A: And what are you going to do?

L: "I'm scared," she replied. "I'm alone and I'm scared."

A: Go ahead and tell me what's going on.

L: I am afraid.

A: What happens when you get close?

L: It is very hot.

I continued to ask questions about that burning house, as I felt I was getting closer to the source of her asphyxiation. The woman in that life kept telling me that she could not put out the fire and that she was out of her house. She kept repeating to me over and over again that it was too hot and that she could not put it out.

A: What else is going on there?

L: I am alone, and I can't walk.

A: Why can't you walk?

L: I am afraid.

A: And can you breathe?

L: "No," she answered, shaking her head from side to side.

A: And why can't you breathe?

L: Because it is very hot.

A: Did people run away?

L: Yes.

A: I want you to go ahead and see what happens.

L: I can't walk and I'm scared. I can't walk.

A: Fast forward in time and tell me if you can get out of there.

L: I can't.

A: And, is the fire coming?

L: Yes.

A: I want you to go ahead and tell me if that's where your body dies. Go ahead. What's going on?

L: She is standing there.

A: Who is standing?

L: Me.

A: What's the matter with you there?

L: I can't move or breathe. The smoke won't let me.

A: Go ahead and tell me if that's where that body dies. Were you able to escape?

L: No. I am asleep.

A: Did you faint?

L: I don't know.

A: Fast forward to the time when you leave the body and if that is where your life ends.

L: "Yes," she answered me in a very soft voice.

A: What do you see when you leave your body?

L: Smoke. My body is lying down and burned. My feet and my dress too.

Once out of the body, I helped her evaluate the life she had just completed in order to have a better understanding of the lessons that had been presented to her. To confirm my suspicions, I asked her the following question:

A: Now that you are out of the body, what else do you see? What else is happening? Where do you decide to go, now that you are a spirit?

L: To the field.

When the body dies, usually the spirit goes to the light or sees other light beings coming for it. In this case, the woman's spirit returned to the field, where she was seeing people running without them perceiving her and seeing a fire whose smoke she could not smell.

As she went back to the moment when she was still outside her house trying to extinguish the flames, she went from not feeling or smelling to doing so, because, until then, she was alive. What we can assume is that, due to the fire and smoke, the woman lost consciousness and died on the spot. This type of death, in a state of unconsciousness, was what caused her confusion, since, when she was in the field near the horses, she had not yet realized that her body had died.

By this time, all that remained was to confirm my suspicions as she gave me the details of that life.

A: Do you see anyone coming for you?

L: No.

A: Do you see any lights?

L: No, I am alone. I am floating.

A: Go ahead and tell me if you ever find the light.

L: I am not afraid anymore.

A: But you haven't gone to the light.

L: No.

A: So, I ask you a question, are you Liliana in a past life or are you attached to Liliana's body?

L: I'm attached.

A: And, at what point did you attach to her?

L: When she was born.

A: And why did you decide to join it?

L: Because I am afraid.

Up to this point, we can deduce that the asphyxia felt by Liliana had been originated by this lost soul, who, consciously or unconsciously, was transmitting to her the agony of her body. The symptom, in reality, was not hers, but that of the woman who died suffocated and burned in that fire. Every time Liliana faced situations in which she felt fear, the symptom of asphyxia was activated.

That day I worked with the woman's spirit so that she could go into the light and elaborate forgiveness for the symptoms she had produced in Liliana, who, after the session, did not experience any more asphyxia. When she came out of the trance, she did not remember anything of what had happened.

Exorcism

Although exorcism is not a concept with which I approach my sessions, I think it is essential to explain why not. The word exorcism comes from the ancient Greek and, later, Romanization *exorkismos*, which literally means 'to compel by oath or conjure', and is understood as the practice of expelling or removing an evil force from a person.

If we define exorcism from a religious point of view, in Catholicism, it consists of a ritual where prayers and expulsion orders are repeated, including the use of objects to repel spirits considered unclean. The Catholic Church bases this practice on the Gospels, where it is narrated how Jesus expelled demons. One such account can be found in the Bible, in Matthew 8:28-34:

28 When he arrived at the other side in the region of the Gadarenes, two demon-possessed men coming from the tombs met him. They were so violent that no one could pass that way

29 "What do you want with us, Son of God?" they shouted. "Have you come here to torture us before the appointed time?"

30 Some distance from them a large herd of pigs was feeding.

31 The demons begged Jesus, "If you drive us out, send us into the herd of pigs."

32 He said to them, "Go!" So they came out and went into the pigs, and the whole herd rushed down the steep bank into the lake and died in the water.

33 Those tending the pigs ran off, went into the town and reported all this, including what had happened to the demon-possessed men.

34 Then the whole town went out to meet Jesus. And when they saw him, they pleaded with him to leave their region.

In the view of the Catholic Church, these are the signs that may indicate possession:

- Aversion to God, the Virgin Mary, the saints, the cross, and sacred images
- Speaking in unfamiliar languages that the subject has not been able to learn on his or her own
- Demonstrate more strength than normal
- Making distant or hidden things present

Some might consider the practice of exorcism as something you see in the movies or that happens on rare occasions, but it would be interesting to read the article that the BBC published on its web portal (www.bbc.com) on April 24, 2018, where it reported that some 250 priests from about 50 countries around the world traveled that month to Rome to learn how to identify demonic possession and learn the rituals to cast out demons. It was the Exorcism and Prayer of Deliverance course, a seminar that the Vatican began to offer in 2005.

My Work: Spiritual Assistance

How do I work with spirits and lost souls in a hypnosis session? I have decided to call this work that I do 'spiritual assistance' because I feel that this is exactly what I do with spirits. I assist not only my client, who could be considered the victim, but also the lost soul, who, if we look at it from another perspective, has also become a kind of victim by being trapped in this dimension.

Contrary to what exorcism does, and following the teachings of my teacher, the Colombian hypnotherapist Aurelio Mejía, my intention is not to expel anyone. I do not use rituals, nor do I repeat prayers, nor do I use objects with supposed powers, much less treat them as unclean spirits. Going a little further, I could say that I do not believe that demons, the devil, or hell exist.

In the years that I have been practicing Introspective Hypnosis, I have only encountered lost souls who claimed to be demons in order to frighten me. In the same way, Aurelio Mejía and José Luis Cabouli, who have a longer track record, have had the same experience as me. They have never encountered one.

My vision of working with spirits comes from love and compassion, based on the concept that we are all sparks of divine light (God). Therefore, that makes us spiritual brothers and sisters and, for that reason alone, any spirit deserves our respect and understanding.

Through my years of study and practice, I have been able to prove, as my teachers taught me, that there are no good or bad spirits, but only spirits that are more evolved than others. When a spirit does something that is catalogued, from the point of view of the human being, as bad, they do it not because they are cruel or heartless, but because they are ignorant. If they knew that what they cause they will have to feel with equal or greater intensity due to the universal law of karma, they would simply not do it. Every lost soul has its own history and its own tragedy. It is the lack of understanding that made them act like that once their body died.

A lost soul attached to my client is like another client and deserves the same respect, dedication, and help in solving his or her problems. There will be times when that soul must also benefit from the various therapeutic techniques we hypnotherapists use. Our goal is to find out their story, to help them remember how their body died, to help them understand why they could not or did not choose to go to the light, and to help them resolve their unresolved issues, even if they are associated with the person to whom they became attached. Finally, we will guide them on the path to the light and, if necessary, ask for assistance from beings of light to guide them to the dimension that corresponds to them.

Coincidentally, what has motivated me to write this book is the misconception—according to my point of view—that exists on this subject. I have seen how some therapists and their hypnosis techniques work with lost spirits as if it were an exorcism without even finding out the background of the situation. For many, the sole purpose of their sessions is for deliverance.

Above we talked about the aura, its function, and the information (signal) it sends to the more subtle dimensions. I believe that, through the aura, spirits and lost souls know what our level of evolution and our intention is when we start working with our clients, and, based on that, they adopt a specific behavior during a session. If they perceive that we are inexperienced or fearful, it is more than certain that they will play with us and seek to give us a hard time. But, if they see that our intention is not to expel them, but to listen to them and give them a hand, their attitude will be totally different; although some will use what I call 'special effects', such as voice changes, gestures, insults, and sudden movements, to dissuade us.

César's Message

I am going to tell you about one of the most transcendental sessions of my career, one that I will carry forever in my heart because it transformed my hypnosis practice, my vision of therapeutic work, and led me to understand my meaning and mission in this reincarnation.

María was a woman from Central America who had gone through many sad and traumatic situations through her mother, who, in revenge to her ex-husband and María's father, did terrible things to her and her brother.

While in trance, she visited a memory in which her mother was assaulting her while other people were trying to defend her. While using the role change technique with her, María let me know that she was feeling a strong pain in her right foot that had not been mentioned during the interview or at the beginning of the session. Thanks to the training I had had with Aurelio Mejía, I understood that it could be a spirit manifesting.

María: My foot hurts.

Antonio: Does your foot hurt?

M: Yes, the right.

A: "Okay, I'm going to take the energy from your right foot and let it express through you. I am taking it. I am taking it into your mind," I touched her forehead and addressed that spirit, "Brother, you can express yourself now. Brother, you can express yourself now. How long have you been with María? A long time or a short time?"

Lost Soul: "A long time," it answered.

A: I understand. So, what happened, brother, why are you with her?

LS: I don't know

A: Are you lost?

LS: I think so.

A: What was your name, brother, were you a man or a woman?

LS: I don't know what I am.

A: Okay, no problem. You are spirit, you are energy. Can you tell me what happened to you? How did you pass to the spiritual plane? How did your body die?

LS: They killed me!

The spirit told me that some men had killed it, but it did not know the reason. I asked it what part of its body hurt when it was killed to find out if it was linked to the ailment María was feeling. "The foot and the heart," it told me.

A: Is there anything that you have caused María voluntarily or involuntarily?

LS: A lot of problems.

A: Like what?

LS: Not to be happy. I don't want her to be happy because I wasn't happy.

After a few more minutes of dialogue, trying to figure out why the spirit was with María and what symptoms it had produced, the spirit told me:

LS: I want to meet Doña Carmen.

A: Doña Carmen the mother or the aunt?

LS: No, the aunt. I need to meet her.

A: Is that the aunt sitting outside?

LS: Yes, the same one.

Carmen was María's aunt and the one who had brought her to the session. At that moment, she was in the waiting room. I asked the spirit to wait a few seconds while I went to get her. When she came into my office, I filled her in on what was going on, letting her know that there was a spirit attached to her niece who wished to speak to her.

Something I realized months after facilitating this session was the fact that two (Raúl and César) of the three spirits attached to María were communicating with me at the same time. Because of this, some of the answers to my questions did not make sense.

LS: Are you Carmen?

Carmen: Yes.

LS: I wanted to meet you.

C: To meet me?

A: Can you explain why?

LS: "Take my hand!" the spirit said in an energetic voice.

Carmen proceeded to take it's hand and the spirit, through María, began to breathe rapidly.

LS: Thank you for being here.

A: Brother, we are here to help you. What can we do for you?

LS: I need to leave your niece alone.

C: Can you tell me who you are?

LS: "Raúl," he said, extending his hand.

C: What Raúl?

LS: Thank you for giving me your hand.

A: What is your relationship with María or Carmen?

LS: "With María, I possessed her," he answered while shaking his head from side to side.

A: Why do you need Carmen if your problem is with María?

LS: "I love Carmen very much. I needed to get to know her through María. I feel like she was my wife," said the spirit, as Carmen smiled nervously.

A: I'm going to count to three, and when I get to three, I want you to go deep into another life and pursue your relationship with Carmen. One, two, three.

LS: I have two children.

A: Two children in that life? Were you male or female?

LS: "I am Carmen's husband," he nodded.

A: What was your name in that life, brother? Was it Raúl?

LS: "No, César. César!" he repeated, raising his voice and the hand Carmen was still holding. "I am Carmen's husband. Where are my children?"

A: César, I am going to explain to you what is going on.

LS: "They killed me!" he said, interrupting me and raising his hand again.

A: That was in another life, brother. What were your children's names?

LS: Juan and Rosa

Little by little, what was happening took on meaning. For the time being, we knew that César had attached to María in order to get to Carmen, who had been his partner in another life.

A: Were you happy with Carmen?

LS: I loved her very much. Through her niece, I found her again.

Carmen was confused, as she did not consciously remember being César's wife in a past life. I asked Carmen if she could understand what was happening and, with a nervous smile, she said yes.

LS: I need to get out of here. I don't want to make María unhappy anymore. I need to let her go.

A: Okay. I'm going to help you in that process, but we need to know what happened, okay?

LS: Okay.

A: You were murdered in that life, do you know why?

LS: Wrongly. I was killed by bad men.

A: Do you forgive those ignorant men who killed your body thinking they were killing your spirit?

LS: "Yes!" he answered, breathing rapidly.

So, we started working with forgiveness therapy to help him free himself from all those negative feelings and emotions. César was grateful that we were with him in this process, while Carmen could not hold back her tears or let go of his hand.

A: So, do you want to apologize to María for the inconvenience you have caused her?

LS: No, not her. Carmen! Forgive me, you don't know, they killed me! Forgive me, please," he begged desperately.

A: She never knew what had happened?

LS: No, she thought I had abandoned them, but they killed me. Please forgive me!

Carmen and I knew that César needed her forgiveness in order to continue on his way. Looking at Carmen, I gestured with my hand and head asking her to follow his conversation as if she understood what he was saying. Actually, I think that, although she was not aware of this, on a subconscious level there was something at work that would help her as well.

C: "Don't worry. Stay calm," Carmen told him in tears.

LS: Forgive me, please. I have loved you very much. I need to get away from here. I don't want to hurt you anymore.

C: Don't worry, I forgive you.

That day, César's lost soul went on its way to the light without first telling us that there were two other lost souls attached to María. Later, in "The Owner of the Wake" I will talk about that second lost soul, and in "The Spirit of a Rapist" I will talk about Raúl, the third one.

There is much to ponder from this session. First, how did César's soul find Carmen, who had already reincarnated in another body? Through his vibratory field, that unique frequency of spirit. César's soul even went further and was able to find a route to reach her, through the vulnerability of his niece to attach to her and thus be close to Carmen waiting for the moment to apologize and explain to her what had really happened with him.

Now, I wonder what would have happened if my focus in the session had only been to free María from César, without even giving him a chance to express himself. What reaction would I have gotten from César if I called him an unclean demon and demanded that he return to the hell he came from? Isn't God love? Isn't one of the commandments of the Catholic religion to love our neighbor as ourselves?

One of the most difficult concepts to explain in the Introspective Hypnosis courses I teach is the loving approach to the session, understanding that what we are doing is helping a reincarnated spirit (our client) to understand who he/she is, but that sooner or later we will also help other disincarnated spirits (lost souls) attached to their aura, waiting to be heard and guided towards the light. It is this empathy with the other that will make a big difference in the final result.

Possession or Attachment?

Spiritual possession is understood as a paranormal phenomenon whereby an evil spirit takes control of its victim's body, causing behavioral changes and a series of physical and psychological symptoms. Usually, possession is attributed to negative energies or demons, who displace their victim's soul to take over his or her body.

Possession cannot be considered a scientific diagnosis, but some attribute symptoms such as schizophrenia, bipolar, epilepsy, hysteria, multiple personality disorder, and subpersonalities as stemming from demonic possession.

In Allan Kardec's *The Spirits' Book*, the spirits say this:

Can a spirit temporarily take over the corporeal envelope of a living person? In other words, can it enter an animate body and replace the spirit incarnated in it?

- A spirit does not enter a body as you enter a house. Instead, it associates with an incarnate spirit who has its same defects and qualities so that they can both act conjointly. Nevertheless, it is always the incarnate spirit who acts upon the matter enveloping it and according to its own wishes. A spirit cannot replace the one who is incarnate because the spirit is connected to the body until the time set for the end of its material existence." The name should be spiritual attachment, which refers to the action that the lost soul performs by attaching itself to the vibratory field of a person. Contrary to the concept of displacement in possession, an attachment is the influence, conscious or unconscious, that a lost soul exerts on the person to whom it has attached itself.

By attaching itself to the person's aura, the lost soul will begin to emit its own signals, information, energy, and frequencies, causing a kind of interference and making the victim of the attachment feel and think the same things it feels and thinks: physical ailments, character changes, fears, sadness, among others. These traits are not really theirs.

The more the lost soul penetrates into the vibratory field of its victim, the more influence it will have on it, and it can reach the point where it is the personality of this parasitic energy that manifests itself almost all the time, giving the impression of a possession (displacement), when it is only a much stronger level of influence.

About this, the spirits contacted in *The Spirits' Book* say:

-If there is no such thing as possession per se, that is, the cohabitation of two spirits in the same body, may a spirit nonetheless find itself dependent on another spirit so that it sees itself "subjugated" or "obsessed" by it to such a degree that its own will is in some way paralyzed?

- "Yes, and these are the truly possessed. You must understand, however, that this kind of domination never occurs without the participation of the one who suffers it, either through weakness or desire. Epileptics and insane individuals have often been taken as being possessed, but they are in need of a doctor rather than an exorcist."

In the regressions to the womb that I have facilitated, where we basically establish the first contact with the spirit before birth, my trance clients have talked to me about the complex process of connecting the soul to the body, integrating it with the brain and the emotional system. So, for me, it is hard to imagine that a spirit can not only attach itself to our vibratory field, but displace us from our body as well.

In the same way, as I have already mentioned, I do not believe in evil or negative spirits, nor in demons, nor in hell. In other words, I do not believe in anything that would make me start a hypnosis session from fear, prejudice, or discrimination towards anyone who needs help, whether they have a body or not.

ENERGIES THAT ARE CONFUSED
WITH PARASITIC SPIRITS

During the course of a hypnosis session, it is possible that our clients may let us know that they are feeling something that is not theirs or that is out of place. This may present as physical pain, headache, pressure in different parts of the body, or as a kind of blockage.

It is not uncommon for them to report these changes themselves since, being in a trance state, their sensitivity is heightened. Basically, a person in an expanded state of consciousness is a medium and may have certain psychic abilities at such times.

There are certain energies stuck together that may give the impression of being lost souls, but, in reality, are not. Does this make any difference to our client? Not really. If a person in a trance state thinks or feels that they have a lost soul attached to them, it makes little difference what we think about it. What matters is what the person feels. We will always treat that energy according to how the individual in trance feels it.

We are not here to find out whether they are right or wrong nor whether or not what they say they are experiencing makes sense. Our goal should always be to make the person feel better by using their internal reality, what they believe and not what does or does not make sense to us.

Let us look at some of the energies that can generate symptoms as if they were a lost soul attached to the person, but probably are not:

Abortions

On several occasions, women who have come to me for a session have expressed with sadness the moment they decided to have an abortion. This may have been because they were not as mature at that age as they are today, because they did not have the financial means, or because their partner had given up on the issue. Whatever the case, the result was always the same: sadness, remorse, and a strong sense of guilt.

Many times, while we were working in the session, they would detect a different sensation in the abdominal area or, when asked to visually scan their energetic body, they would see a shadow in that area. Was it the spirit of the unborn fetus? To answer this question, I would like to refer to the work of the American physician and psychiatrist Brian Weiss.

When I read his book *Only Love Is Real*, I didn't know anything about hypnosis yet, but I was struck by the part where he talked about Pedro and Elizabeth. Pedro was sad because a partner he had had decided to abort the child they were expecting together, making him feel guilty too. Weiss told him that he should not feel that way because, in fact, at that moment the spirit of their child was not yet there, but Pedro didn't understand what he meant. Apparently, Weiss was already aware that the spirit does not occupy his future body until much later in the pregnancy.

Now, if we refer to the work of Michael Newton in his books *Destiny of Souls* and *Life Between Lives*, we will find the same answer in the enormous amount of regressions to the womb that he carried out. His patients reported the process of integration with the baby's body as described by Sabrina in her session with me, of whom I spoke above.

Having said all this, and assuming that the miscarriage or loss occurred during the first months of pregnancy, when it is very likely that the soul has not been integrated into the fetus yet, what do these women feel in the womb? As we are creative and manifesting beings, it is very likely that all those negative feelings that they felt and currently feel have been converted into energy attached to that area, which would also cause them discomfort and problems.

In such cases, I have them communicate with that energy as if it were the baby's lost soul. I have them explain why they made the decision to abort. I ask the baby's soul if it blames its mother for making that decision at a difficult time in their life—although the answer is always no—and I let the mother work out the forgiveness and then send the supposed lost soul into the light.

This dynamic brings closure to that painful chapter for women, and I have found that it always works for my clients. If something imaginary could make us sick, why could something imaginary not also help us heal?

By this I do not mean that it is not possible for a soul already integrated into the fetus to decide to adhere to the vibratory field of its mother, but many times it is the mother who creates the trauma due to her emotions.

Multiple Personality Disorder and Subpersonalities

Also called dissociative identity disorder, multiple personality disorder is a mental illness that causes a disconnection between actions, thoughts, memories, environment, and identity.

Among the symptoms of dissociative identity disorder we have:

- Amnesia regarding certain events or time periods
- Separation from oneself
- Perception of people and things in the environment
- Inability to cope with emotional stress
- Depression and anxiety

Among the main reasons are traumatic events such as sexual abuse, emotional abuse, or torture.

Treatment aims to control symptoms, stabilize the individual, seek integration of personalities, and, finally, regain identity.

On the other hand, subpersonalities are a personality mode that is activated to enable the individual to cope with certain psychosocial situations. This form of personality may include feelings, emotions, actions, and other elements of human behavior.

It is not uncommon for both pathologies to be mistaken for one or more lost souls attached to the individual. Although treatment for multiple personalities resembles the process of spiritual assistance in that both focus on finding the source of the symptom in order to eliminate it, the two differ in that one seeks to integrate the personalities, while spiritual assistance seeks to help the lost soul go to the light and detach from the person.

Thought Forms

It is a projection of the consciousness of another reincarnated spirit (another person) in which negative emotions are formed, such as anger, sadness, revenge, and obsession, which ends up attaching to the vibratory field of the victim, just as a lost soul does, and basically generating the same problems. The only big difference is that the owner of that thought is still on Earth and, therefore, cannot be sent to the light.

I still remember the case of Johanna, a young girl of about seventeen years, whom her mother brought to my house to work on different symptoms. During the interview, she told me that her father was a physical trainer and that he and her mother had been separated for years. Every time Johanna went to visit her father, the first thing he did before even greeting her was to tell her, "you are getting fat. Watch your weight, you are getting fat." The truth is that I did not see her as overweight, but that was the perception and trauma that her father was creating in her little by little.

During the last phase of the session, I asked her to do a visualization of her vibratory field to tell me if she saw anything out of place. Not surprisingly, she detected a kind of shadow in her abdominal area. I brought her mind to that energy for her to express herself. When I asked the shadow to identify herself, she told me it was her father. It was basically the projection of his consciousness and obsession with his daughter not gaining weight.

I began to dialogue with that part of her consciousness, just as I would have done with an attached spirit, and once forgiveness was worked out, I asked her to return to her body. So, what was it that created that stuck thought form in Johanna's vibrational shift? Her father's obsession with her not gaining weight.

I have also seen this type of obsession during the breakup of a relationship, whether it is an estrangement or a divorce. The victim of this circumstance begins to experience symptoms shortly after separation. The common denominator in those cases is that the other person did not accept the breakup of the relationship, generating an obsession and a way of thinking that stuck to my client.

Walk-Ins

The first time I heard this term was in Dolores Cannon's texts and, although so far, I have not come across one of them, the concept is a little difficult for me to accept. It is said that a walk-in is a spirit that will occupy or is occupying a body that did not originally belong to it, that is to say, that the soul that is the original owner of the body leaves and returns to the light, giving up the post to another spirit that will occupy it and continue its life. It is even said that the new spirit that enters the body will keep the memories and everything lived by the previous spirit, even if the personality changes.

But what is the purpose of this? Cannon explains that there are times when the spirit, before it is born, chooses more lessons than it can take and, realizing that it is too much for it, decides that it wants to return to the light, but without committing suicide. It is then that this spirit makes a contract with another to continue the life of that body, assuming that this body fulfills the objectives of the lessons that this new spirit needs to learn.

It is quite confusing. Under the same logic that integrating the soul into the body in the womb is a process that takes time, this could not be possible. How can a spirit detach itself from the body just like that for another to enter?

The concept of walk-in was also used by William Baldwin in his book *Spirit Releasement Therapy*, where he mentions that the term was first used in 1979 by journalist and psychic Ruth Montgomery.

Michael Newton says in his book *Life Between Lives* that he has never come across one and that he himself finds the idea hard to believe. Moreover, I have not heard Aurelio Mejía talk about this subject either. If I mention it in this book it is because many hypnotherapists use this terminology and talk to their clients about it. On the other hand, many people who come to a hypnosis session say they believe they are a walk-in, or perhaps they just have questions about it.

Implants

By implants I mean energetic and not necessarily physical ones. Implants are energetic devices supposedly placed by extraterrestrials in our vibratory field with different intentions. It is said that some are to be able to know our location, others to collect data that will later be studied by them, and a few to control our energy level. Anyway, I have heard all kinds of explanations and reasons why a human being could have one.

Some people say they agreed to lend themselves to studies before reincarnating, several do not remember, and others have a conversation with these beings during the trance, trying to understand why they have it.

The way I handle these cases is basically by respecting the free will that human beings have. I ask the person if they want to keep it or not. If they want to remove it, I ask them to visualize a white light dissolving it. Some therapists give the suggestion to their client that they are pulling it out by placing their hands on the area where they have visualized it. Others even ask you to call the being who placed it on you and instruct them to remove it at this time as they should not interfere with our free will.

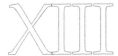

SPIRITS IN HYPNOSIS

In the history of hypnosis, there are many people whose work and research have helped the evolution of this discipline. In this chapter, based on the influence they have had on my own practice, I will mention a few of them.

As I mentioned at the beginning of this book, hypnotic trance has been used since Ancient Egypt in the temples of sleep, or dream temples, to treat ailments of psychological origin. Later, one would hear of the German physician Franz Anton Mesmer (1734 -1815) and 'mesmerism', a therapy based on the use of magnets for the healing of his patients. He believed that the body had a universal fluid that could be artificially controlled through magnets that helped to heal.

Later, the French aristocrat Armand de Chastenet (1751-1825) and Marquis of Puységur, was able to recreate what Mesmer did with his patients, finding that the person was not asleep during the hypnotic state, but entered a kind of somnambulism. He determined this when a 23-year-old man, named Victor Race, was able to answer his questions while in a trance. He decided to call this technique 'artificial somnambulism' or 'magnetic somnambulism'.

A few years later, the Scottish neurosurgeon James Braid (1795 - 1860) would become the pioneer of the use of hypnosis as anesthesia. Braid, who disagreed with Mesmer's theory of 'mesmerism', recognized the veracity of the phenomenon, but also believed that it was based on suggestion. He determined that all hypnosis is self-hypnosis, i.e., that no operator is needed to achieve this state.

Later, the American psychiatrist and psychologist Milton Erickson (1901 - 1980) specialized in the medical use of hypnosis and family therapy, founding the American Society of Clinical Hypnosis. Erickson used metaphors to induce his patients into psychoemotional situations without losing consciousness. He maintained that the individual does not relate to the world through their senses, but rather through their internal maps, and that is why there are no inappropriate behaviors since these correspond to a reaction to his internal reality.

Trance and Expanded States of Consciousness

There are three components of the mind with certain functions: the conscious mind, the subconscious mind, and the critical mind.

The **conscious mind** is the area where the critical mind, reason, logic, and willpower are located. It is basically our analytical part, whose function—in my opinion—is to ensure the survival of our body. It protects us from any event that may overload us, extracting it and sending it to the subconscious mind until we are ready to deal with it.

In the **subconscious mind**, our associations, both positive and negative, as well as our internal maps are stored. For example, those who smoke cigarettes may relate the feeling of relaxation to this vice and those who drink alcohol may relate it to a disconnection from reality.

As the subconscious part occupies approximately 88% of our mind, whatever we embrace there will always have more influence over what we consciously desire.

Remembering what Milton Erickson, renowned American physician and hypnotherapist, said, it is through these stored associations that we relate to the world. What is in the subconscious mind is our purest reality, the one that dictates how we behave in life and how we react to certain situations because, whether we remember it or not, we have associations there created during traumatic events that the conscious mind wished to remove to protect us.

How is information recorded in the subconscious? According to what I have been able to appreciate with my own clients, it is through three ways: by trauma, by repetition, or by visualization.

In my sessions, as I help my clients search for the origin of their fears, several of them go back to the time when their parents repeated over and over again that they could get hurt riding a bicycle, playing sports, running, or jumping. In the end, the fear they felt did not belong to them, but to their parents, who had engraved it in their subconscious after repeating the same thing over and over again.

What is stored in the subconscious is usually distorted because it was not recorded according to what actually happened. Before any event reaches this area of the mind, it goes through a filter that contemplates our belief system, memories, past decisions, metaprograms, values, and basic needs.

Moreover, from the point of view of regressive hypnosis and spirituality, it is understood that what we have stored in our subconscious does not correspond only to what happened in the space of time in which we have been in this body. In our subconscious we also keep memories, associations, and traumas of the bodies we have occupied in other lives.

On the other hand, the **critical mind** is located between the conscious and subconscious areas, acting as a kind of guardian or password that we must enter into a computer before we can store and extract information from it. It is the one that decides what passes and what does not pass to the subconscious mind.

When we are children, the critical mind is not yet well developed and everything that happens to us goes directly to the subconscious, easily creating a memory or a negative circumstance. That is why most of the traumas we carry as adults originated in our childhood.

***

Having understood the components of the human mind, let us now define hypnotic trance. It is a state of reverie, where the individual is between asleep and awake, and is highly susceptible to suggestions.

This is a natural human state as we all go through it at least twice a day: before waking up and before falling asleep. In both moments, it is as if we were watching a movie in which we get so involved in the plot that we can be moved to tears. If, while driving our car, we realize that we should have turned right three blocks back, then we were in a trance. We were driving the car ourselves, but we were focused on something else.

How Does a Person Go Into a Trance?

All hypnosis is self-hypnosis. The hypnotist or hypnotherapist can give a series of instructions that we call inductions, but it is up to us to follow them or not to reach that state. Our collaboration is required, and no one can force us.

Inductions come in different types. Some can last from 7 to 15 minutes, seeking a relaxation of the body; a few, which are considered quick inductions, are less than 4 minutes, such as Dave Elman's induction; and, others are considered instantaneous inductions, such as the shock- or pattern-interruption induction.

Be that as it may, the objective of the inductions is to go through the critical mind in order to have direct access to the subconscious. This would be the equivalent of when a *hacker* enters our computer to gain access to all our information.

But how can this be possible? Simple. The critical mind is the one that analyzes and protects us. If I were to just look a person in the eye and say "go to sleep", they would think I was crazy because they don't have to go to sleep just because I tell them to. This is just the critical mind doing its job. But, if I distract the conscious and critical mind by giving them a task, such as looking at the dot in my hand, this will allow me to speak directly to the subconscious mind, which is always attentive, as Milton Erickson said, and will act according to the suggestion given to it, allowing it to go into trance.

Can We Only Enter Trance by Means of an Induction?

The altered state of consciousness is natural in human beings. We experience it when we fall asleep, in that middle point between asleep and awake, when we are walking in the supermarket and we realize that we forgot to put in a product we wanted, when we cross a few steps behind, or when we see a movie and we cry when we get sucked into the plot.

During the sessions I facilitate, I use José Luis Cabouli's Past Life Therapy technique and ask questions about each client's symptom or emotion while the client has their eyes closed. While defining the symptom, which we will then locate in some part of the body as if associating it with something known, we are helping the person to become conscious of what up to that moment is unconscious to them: the origin of the symptom in a possible past life.

By working in this way, the person begins to enter into an expanded state of consciousness without the need for any induction.

Myths About Hypnosis

There are many myths and misconceptions about hypnosis. In the long run, these only provoke an unfounded fear in the individual who needs a session. Among these myths, we have:

- Hypnosis is falling asleep
- I can lose control during the trance state
- The hypnotist needs special powers
- I may not wake up
- It is something diabolical
- I can be abused
- I won't remember anything when I come out of the trance

All these beliefs are far from reality. Hypnosis is an altered state of consciousness and, therefore, we are conscious at all times. No one can lose control of themselves so they will not do anything that goes against their principles. Nor are you at the mercy of the hypnotist or hypnotherapist.

In addition, it is common to remember everything that happened while in trance. Some people will only retain small fragments of what happened, but only 3% will go to what we call the somnambulistic level, where they will not remember anything that happened.

In hypnosis we work with the subconscious, but, in my case, most of the time I work directly with the spirit of my client, who is the one who stores all the information.

States of Mind

Our brain produces electrical impulses known as brain waves. These contain information that travels from neuron to neuron to perform a particular function. There are four main types of brain waves:

- Beta: produced when we are awake and alert.

- Alpha: these are generated when we are in a state of relaxation, with our eyes closed or resting. It is a state similar to meditation and facilitates visualization.

- Theta: this a deeper state of relaxation. It is when we are almost asleep and allows us to visualize even more.

- Delta: these originate while we are asleep.

When we go into a trance state, we go from beta to alpha and, depending on how deep we can go in that trance, we can reach the theta level, where we will hardly remember what will happen during that phase. As I said before, only 3% of people get there.

Our brain and mind will go to the level of trance necessary to work during the session, but it is not necessary to reach the theta state to be able to perceive spirits and lost souls or to work on other matters during the session.

What Happens When We Are in a Trance and What is it Used for?

A person in trance, contrary to popular belief, will be in an altered state of consciousness in which their senses will be heightened, i.e., they will be able to access memories that they could not access consciously.

Having put aside the conscious mind, which is the one that analyzes and filters, we will have free access to everything that is stored in the subconscious to analyze it from objectivity and not from what our personal filters have interpreted. But, mainly, a person in that state will have access to a more subtle dimension—at least that is how I understand it—where time and space do not exist. It could be said that this can enter the same dimension where we develop as spirits before reincarnating.

In the space of "no time"—as I call it—, everything happens now and that is where you can interact from the present, even though, under the concept of linear time, that event is considered past. Working from that space gives me a lot of flexibility with my clients during a session. On the other hand, when the person is in this expanded state of consciousness, they can see, feel, and perceive more; not only their environment, but also their body and emotions.

It is coincidentally in this state that the spirits attached to the energetic field can no longer hide and begin to manifest themselves in different ways. Another thing that often happens during a trance is that people can perceive the presence of other spirits that are not necessarily attached to them, but only come closer to engage in communication, as is the case of deceased loved ones or other spirits that will simply try to take the opportunity to dialogue.

THE SPACE OF 'NO TIME' AND
THE SPIRITS OF LOVED ONES

One of the saddest moments for human beings is during the departure of our loved ones. That sorrow is based on the idea that the person died when, in reality, what died was their body, but not their spirit, since it is eternal.

Many times, these feelings make us unable to see that their spirit is well, that they are no longer suffering—depending on how they passed away—and even that they want to say goodbye to us before they go to the light. At that moment, we are so immersed in that grief and our mind is so busy thinking about everything that has just happened, that we do not have the tranquility to receive their presence and what they want to transmit to us.

When one of my clients visits these types of memories, I use quantum time, which has the premise that there is no past, present, or future; that the spirit does not understand the body and that, for the spirit, every-thing is happening now. So, speaking in linear time, the death of a loved one may have taken place some years ago, but, as they are in a trance and has returned to that event, for them it is happening in the present. Under that understanding, they can even accompany the soul of their loved one during the process of the death of their body and, as the trance allows my client to be in an expanded state of consciousness, they will be able to process that event from another perspective, seeing everything that happens from the spiritual dimension.

It took me a while to understand these concepts, but, as I explained a few pages ago, conducting a session from the idea that everything happens now is what has allowed me to have excellent results in my hypnosis sessions.

Giovanna and Grandmother

To better explain linear time and quantum time, I will talk about the session of Giovanna, who came to my office with the purpose of treating certain psychosomatic symptoms, including back pain and sadness.

First, we navigate through a couple of sad memories from her childhood: when she was bullied at school by her classmates for having big cheeks and when she had an incident on her way home from school as a teenager.

The next event we visited was related to the death of her grandmother, whom she called mom because she had raised her since she was a child. This caused me confusion because I knew her mother was still alive, in fact, she was in another room of the house during the session. To dispel my doubts, I had to ask her a couple of questions to make sure this was not related to a past life.

Antonio: Let's look for another memory, one that bothered you, one that made you sad. Five, four, three, two, one. You are already there.

At that moment, Giovanna's face was flooded with sadness and she began to cry.

A: I see you found it. At that moment that you are reliving, is it day or night?

G: It is daytime.

A: What is happening?

G: We are burying...

A: Who are they burying?

G: "My mom," she said crying.

A: What is your mother's name?

G: Leti. Leticia.

A: How old are you there?

G: Twenty-two years.

A: "And do you know a lady named Celia," I asked her trying to find out if this event was from this life or a previous one.

G: Yes, it's my mom.

A: Then why are you telling me that the mother they are burying is Leticia?

G: She is my grandmother.

A: I see. It's about your grandmother, who was like your mother. What else is going on? Are they at the funeral?

G: "I want to go with my mom," she exclaimed between sobs, shaking her head from side to side. "Mom, take me. Please take me."

A: Let me explain something to you What has died is your grandmother's body. Your grandmother is a spirit and she is not dead. I'm going to prove it to you. I'm going to count from three to one and you are going to greet her. Three, two, one. Say hello to your grandmother.

G: "Mom," she exclaimed with joy. "My old lady."

A: Communication is mental and telepathic. What is coming into your mind? What is your grandmother telling you? How is she feeling?

G: "She says she's fine," she replied with a smile.

A: Of course. You see? Since communication is open, take advantage of it and tell your grandmother everything you've wanted to tell her all this time.

G: "She is always with me. I know she is always with me. Yes, mom," she said, beginning the dialogue with her. "I miss her a lot when I go and don't see her."

A: Ask her if she is aware of all the events that have occurred in your family since she passed on, since we will all leave someday because we are spirit.

G: She says yes.

A: May I speak to her?

G: Yes.

A: "Very good. Let her express herself through your mind. One, two, three," I said, touching her forehead. "Mrs. Leticia, good afternoon. Thank you for the communication."

Leticia: Good afternoon.

A: We are helping your granddaughter Giovanna to heal, and I want to know if we can count on your support.

L: Yes.

A: Thank you very much. I would like to know if there is any advice you would like to give to your granddaughter.

L: Love your children very much.

At that moment, I could tell that Grandma had started a mental conversation with Giovanna. I asked them to please repeat what they were talking about out loud so I could find out what they were saying.

G: Oh, my pretty old lady. Yes, mom.

A: What is she telling you?

G: "That I am her favorite granddaughter. I know, Mom," she nodded her head in agreement, as she continued to mentally converse with her grandmother.

A: Can you repeat back to me what she says so that it is on the recording?

G: To take good care of me, to love José (her husband). Yes, I know, mommy. I know, mommy.

A: Can you repeat what she says?

G: "That she loved my children very much, that I should take good care of them, that not everything people tell me is true or a lie, that I should not believe people. She also asks me to take good care of my aunt Celia (her mother)," she told me smiling. "Yes, mom. Don't scold me. Yes, I know she is my mother, but I love you very much. Yes, not my Aunt Cassie. I love her very much too."

A: What are you saying about Aunt Cassandra?

G: That she's a stubborn, stubborn woman. My Aunt Cassie? Huh? I don't understand her. I don't understand her at all.

A: Is she gesturing? Try to mimic what she is saying.

G: What? No! No, no, no, no, I don't understand anything you are telling me.

A: Is what she shows you an image or a noise?

G: It is a noise.

L: The aunt envies the tranquility that this little girl has. Don José has already told her that he wants to see her rolling. What a pity that my own daughter....

A: And can you help them get along better?

L: They get along well, but Cassie doesn't understand. Oh, my little girl!

A: Do you know the origin of the headaches she has?

L: "If I am not mistaken, it is an evil that was coming for me," she answered, referring to some witchcraft.

A: Does Giovanna believe in witchcraft?

L: She doesn't believe. She doesn't believe at all.

A: So, would you help us remove that headache she has?

L: Yes, my daughter has to be healthy. She deserves it very much.

Up to this point we had communicated with Giovanna's grandmother. What had started with a sad memory, such as the death of a loved one, was turning into a beautiful dialogue in which both had the opportunity to tell each other everything they needed. Doña Leticia had even been able to give her granddaughter advice about her life and about some of her relatives.

Many might say that this conversation could have been created by Giovanna's mind. But whether it was imaginary or not, from the point of view of therapeutic work, this should not matter since what is sought is a positive result: transforming a sad event into a joyful and beautiful one.

But, in the same way, I will demonstrate why we should believe that this communication was real: first, Giovanna showed joy at seeing her grandmother appear in front of her; second, the gestures, emotions, and tone of voice changed when one spoke and then the other; third, at one point in the dialogue, the grandmother said something that Giovanna could not understand no matter how hard she tried; and, fourth, the grandmother began to speak about Giovanna in the third person.

That is not all. That conversation between grandmother and grand-daughter continued for several more minutes, reinforcing the idea that what was happening was 100% true.

A: Shall we take away the headache? That doesn't let her move forward and she doesn't need it anymore, does she?

L: No, this child does not need any of the symptoms that she has.

A: Can you help me take all that away?

L: Yes.

A: Because she also mentioned to me that she has problems with her energy. It's like she's more down than usual.

L: Yes, I know where all that comes from.

A: Waist pain too?

L: "Yes," she replied, nodding her head.

A: Can you help me remove all that?

Quickly, the grandmother began to work on Giovanna's body. I could tell because she was gesturing as if she was visualizing something. Meanwhile, I was having a friendly conversation with her, asking her questions about the origin of her granddaughter's fears and her lack of self-esteem, and she was sending messages to her relatives.

When I asked her if her granddaughter was ready, she replied:

L: "She is in pain," she said, looking down at her granddaughter's body.

A: Where?

L: At the waist.

A: That's what she told me. Can you help me take it off?

L: No.

A: Does she have anything there?

L: Yes.

A: Any shadows? I asked, referring to an attached spirit.

L: No.

A: What does she have?

L: "It's something…" she answered, pausing as she moved her head down to look at the body. "No, she has to go to the doctor."

A: Is it something you need to worry about and not delay?

L: Yes, it has to be fast. Very fast.

A: And once it is solved, do you help us from there?

L: My daughter has to go fast, very, very fast. It's practically an emergency.

A: What else are you seeing?

L: It's her back. No one believes her feelings, but my little girl is sick.

A: Tell her what it is so that when she goes to the doctor, she can say check this and check that.

L: No, the doctors already have a result. This girl is stubborn. She has to go fast. If possible, as soon as she gets out of here.

After talking with her grandmother for a few more minutes and receiving that warning, I proceeded to bring Giovanna out of her trance. When she opened her eyes, she only remembered the beautiful communication with her grandmother, but she did not remember anything else that had taken place.

A few days later, I called Giovanna to check on her. She told me that she had seen a doctor, as recommended by her grandmother, and that he had found tumors. Her surgery was scheduled in a couple of days.

Grandma had been right and that is why she had recommended she to go to the doctor urgently.

How and When Can the Tool of 'No Time' Be Used?

There are many ways in which I use the concept of 'no time' to have a conversation with the spirits of my clients' loved ones.

The intention is not to use the client as a medium or to establish a communication to ask questions as if it were an oracle. Nor do I believe that the sole purpose for someone to have a hypnosis session with me is to have a rapprochement with their deceased loved one, even though many have asked me to do so. The opportunity presents itself. If there is something to work through in grief or bereavement, my client's spirit, which is wise, will lead them there. It is at that point that I take the opportunity to engage in a dialogue if we are allowed to do so.

In conclusion, I believe that the idea of 'no time' can be used on certain, specific occasions:

- The person goes to the moment when their loved one has died or is dying: If the client relives the dying phase, I give them instructions to help them become aware of what is happening to the body and to assist them until they leave this plane.

  Why is it important for them to be aware of what is happening to their body? To avoid the entrapment of the soul post mortem. Once out of the body, a dialogue can be established where they can tell each other everything that was left pending before leaving for the light.

- If the sadness that the individual brings to the session is that they were unable to say goodbye to their loved one: This usually occurs when the person was unable to say goodbye because they were far away. I have had many of these cases, especially immigrants who received the news that a family member passed away and could not be by their side.

  What I do in this case is to explain to them that, during the trance state, there are no limits of time or space. I ask them to imagine that their spirit leaves their body and flies to where that family member is at the time of their departure. The procedure is similar to the one described in the previous point.

- When you come to a memory where a deceased loved one is still alive: I am not necessarily referring to the moment of their death, for it may even be a few years earlier.

  We can interact with that spirit in another scenario and establish a communication so that they can tell each other what they need to tell each other, even though we know that at the present time that person is no longer there. I know it may sound confusing, but the truth is that the spirit is the same and is in a 'no time' dimension where everything is happening now.

Father of the Bride

To better explain this last point, I will share the session of Marisel, who took my Introspective Hypnosis course a few years ago.

During her childhood, Marisel had experienced several painful events that she had ended up blocking out. This was a defense mechanism that her mind had chosen to employ to avoid suffering. At the beginning of the session, when she tried to go back in time to those sad memories, she presented some mental blockages.

In order not to insist or frustrate her, I asked her to move to a happy memory. Easily, she arrived at her wedding day, where her father, who was now dead, was present. I thought, then, that in order to get Marisel to visit those memories that her mind was trying to forget, I could ask for her father's help, using the concept of 'no time'.

A: Three, two, one. You are there, Marisel. Tell me what comes into your head.

M: "I'm dancing," she said with a smile.

A: How old are you there?

M: Twenty-four. It's my wedding day with David and my dad is there too.

A: So, how do you feel?

M: "Happy. Everyone is here," she replied, visibly emotional.

A: And what else is going on?

M: Everyone is dancing and laughing. There are a lot of them. My dad is quiet because he says he is leaving, but we are all happy.

This last piece of information let me know that there was already a communication going on between them on a spiritual level, because, at her wedding, she did not know that her father would die soon.

A: And why do you think your dad is quiet?

M: Because he is thinking that he will leave soon.

A: And where will he go?

M: "To unite with the universe. He is looking at me," she told me with tears in her eyes.

A: Since time doesn't exist and everything happens now, ask your dad why he is so quiet.

M: Because he knows he won't be seeing us physically anytime soon.

A: He has spoken a great truth, for he has remarked that this is only in a physical form. The body is just a biological suit that we, the spirits, use to be on this planet. Ask your dad to go forward in time and tell you if, once he is a spirit, he will still be able to see you.

M: He says yes.

A: So, ask your dad, who is a spirit now, how he is doing.

M: He is in union with the universe.

A: Then, from that union with the universe, ask him if he has any advice or message for you.

M: "I am always close to you," she said, repeating what her father was telling him.

A: You see? So why are you sad if he is always near you? What we have to do is not only pay attention to the physical body, but also feel the spirit, the energy. Ask your dad if he is aware of everything that has happened in your life since he left, since he went ahead of us.

M: He says yes.

A: And what can he tell you about your life, about the decisions you are making?

M: "I'm proud of you. You're doing well," she said repeating her father's message.

A: Would you lend him your mind and lips to communicate with me?

M: Yes.

A: I'm going to count to three and you change. Three, two, one. Switch. Floyd, good evening, thank you for the communication.

Floyd: "Good evening," he said in the softest, slowest voice.

A: Floyd, I have some questions to ask you to help Marisel, could you answer them for me?

F: "Yes," he answered, as Marisel's eyelids moved faster indicating a deeper trance.

A: Floyd, Marisel tells me that she doesn't remember anything from her childhood until she was nine years old. However, she now mentioned to me two happy memories from when she was four and five. Do you know why she has blocked her memories?

F: Her mother and I were arguing in front of the two girls.

A: And do you think that because of that she blocked those memories?

F: Yes, because she didn't like it.

A: Floyd, tell me, are you in the light?

F: Yes.

A: And, from the light, how could you help me help Marisel remember all those years? There is valuable information she should have in that age range. We all need that part of our identity. I understand that she may have experienced sad events, but, if we teach her to change the perception of what happened and help her to remove that negative emotion, maybe we will help her to remember everything else, what do you think?

F: Yes.

It was thus, with Floyd's help, that we were able to go back to the events of Marisel's childhood, where there was unfinished business. It was her own father who guided us to work on them.

Goodbye, Brother

Susan wanted to find out about the mental blocks she had, as well as resolve several questions about her life. One of the things that affected her the most was not being able to tell John, her deceased brother, how much she loved him and how proud she was of him.

John had died from a gunshot wound. Apparently, this had happened in front of Susan, making this event even more traumatic and painful for her. Already in a trance, she moved back to that tragic moment.

Antonio: Five, four, three, two, one. You're already there. Tell me what's going on.

Susan: "I see him lying on the ground," she replied, moving her eyes. "He's by his truck, trying to hang on."

A: What else is going on? I want you to connect with that emotion. If you feel like crying, let the tears come out.

S: "He is tired," she said very emotionally.

A: Is he injured?

S: Yes, he is tired of fighting.

A: How does that make you feel?

S: I think he should fight to be here.

A: Keep telling me everything you see.

S: He doesn't move. It's like he's giving up. He wants to rest.

A: "Go a little deeper now," I indicated by putting my hand on her shoulder. "Move to the moment he rests. What's going on?"

S: How can he be happy and not be here with us?

This phrase implied to me that Susan was seeing the spirit of her brother, who had just left his body. She was perceiving more than she had originally seen when that event first occurred.

Being in a trance, she had access to the subtle dimension where spirits dwell, where time does not exist, where she could be with her brother once again. It didn't matter that the event had taken place some years ago.

A: Let's find out. What just died is your brother's body. It is like the clothes we spirits wear on this planet, but he is spirit. Ask him if he is sad or if he is happy.

S: He is happy.

A: Ask him why.

S: "He says they are friendly," she replied, referring to other spirits.

A: Who are friendly?

S: The people (the spirits).

A: Can you lend your mind and lips to John to talk to him?

S: Yes.

A: Very good. One, two, three, connect. John, good morning, are you Susan's brother?

John: Yes.

A: Thank you for the communication, John. Do you realize that your sister is sad because she doesn't understand what just happened? Do you want to explain to her what happened?

J: "I was beaten up by some people and I didn't want to go back. There is a lot of pressure here," he said, referring to Earth.

A: When you say you didn't want to go back, do you mean back to the body?

J: Yes.

A: Are you well and happy where you are?

J: Yes, I am.

A: Susan feels guilty for not being able to express how much she loved and cares for you. Susan, this is the time to tell him. He is spirit and has always been with you.

S: I'm sorry for not showing you as much love as I should have, but I love you and I want you to know that I will always be here for you.

A: John, did you always know this?

J: "Yes," he replied, changing his tone of voice and sighing.

A: Do you think she should regret not having been able to express her love for you before you left?

J: No.

A: What do you want to tell her about it?

J: It's all right. I already knew you loved me. I made certain choices in my life, but I knew how you felt about me.

When I facilitate a communication between loved ones, I also often ask for advice for my client, in addition to asking questions related to the issues that came up in the session.

As I explained earlier, I do not want to use this approach to make predictions or ask frivolous questions that do not make any sense from the point of view of the spiritual dimension. The questions I ask are oriented to help the person in their evolution, especially if they have any misconceptions or misperceptions that may be blocking them.

J: Be at peace. I'm fine.

A: To close the circle, do you have permission to tell him if you are going to be together in a future life?

J: Yes, we will be.

A: Would you mind if I ask you a few questions to give me a hand in helping your sister?

J: No.

A: Okay. She feels depression and anxiety, where does that come from?

J: She is sensing things from others around her.

A: So it's not her. It's just that she's empathetic. Could you help us balance her energy so she doesn't feel that way?

J: Yes. She needs to meditate more.

A: What would she achieve by meditating more?

J: She will be able to focus her energy when she receives those feelings. She will know how to redirect them, how to handle them.

A: Does any of that have to do with your death?

J: No.

A: What else can you tell her?

J: Relax a little.

A: She is so concerned about her future and her career, she wants to be told what is the next step she should take. What can you tell her about that?

J: She has many talents. She can do many other things. She just has to decide what she wants to do.

A: It's always up to her, right?

J: Yes.

A: No one is going to tell her what to do.

J: No.

Thus, using the concept of 'no time', Susan had the opportunity to tell her brother everything she had not been able to tell him when he still had a body.

In that session, John gave his sister a lot of reassurance and, even better, gave her advice to do what she wanted to do using her talents. What she had previously considered a sad memory became a beautiful communication full of love and hope.

A Mother's Love

I will share another segment of Sophia's session, who came to my office to find the root of a chronic back pain she had been experiencing for the past few years. An early part of Sophia's session is found in "Thrown from a Balcony."

That afternoon she was able to communicate with her mother's spirit. During the session, Sophia relived a tragic scene from her past, when, one night, her cousin knocked on her door to tell her that her mother had died. She felt very sad and guilty because she had not called her mother that night.

Sophia: "I have to go see her," she exclaimed in desperation. "I need to see my mom."

Antonio: Go see your mother and tell me everything that is happening.

S: "They won't let me in," she answered, bursting into tears, "They tell me no."

A: Do you want to see your mom?

S: Yes.

A: Remember that you are spirit. Are you inside the house?

S: No, I'm at the front door and there are people standing there that I don't know. I want to see her and they won't let me in. I want to hug her and tell her I'm sorry, that I couldn't call her.

A: I'm going to count from three to one. When I get to number one, I want you to get out of your body and fly to where your mother is. Three, two, one. Fly. Fly to your mom and tell me what's going on.

S: She is standing on a cloud.

A: Very good. How does she look?

S: Beautiful.

A: What color is her energy?

S: Purple.

A: Then tell her everything you have wanted to tell her. You were worried about her body when she was already spirit.

S: I have been good. I've been good to people. I didn't become bad. I help people, mom.

A: What does your mom tell you?

S: "She's kissing me on the forehead," she said, crying.

A: So, hug your mom.

S: She is wonderful.

A: Ask her if she knows what just happened to her, to her body.

S: Yes, she does.

A: Ask her if she is ready to go to the light, where she belongs.

S: "She says yes. But, I don't want her to go. I want her to stay," she said, crying inconsolably.

At that point, I had to explain to Sophia that not letting her go was like being sad that the prisoner she had shared her cell with for years had already served her sentence. It was time to go home. She should be happy that her partner was finally free.

A: "What should we do when we love someone," I asked.

S: Let them go.

A: That's it! Very good. But, before she leaves, tell her everything you've wanted to tell her all along.

S: "I love you, I love you, I love you," she said between tears and shaking her head. "I'm sorry for having caused you so much pain, for not knowing how to behave. I didn't know what to do."

A: Why don't you ask your mom if you should feel sorry about that?

S: She says no, that I was a child.

A: May I talk to your mom for a moment? I'm going to count from three to one. When I get to one, lend her your mind and lips. Three, two, one. Norma, good morning. Thank you for the communication.

Norma: "Hello," she said in a softer tone of voice.

A: You can see that your daughter is sad because your body died. She feels that she is left behind and some remorse. What can we say to her to put her mind at ease?

N: That my spirit will never leave her. I am always here. That I love her and that she never did anything wrong. She grew up.

A: So why do you feel guilty?

N: I don't know. She has a heart of gold and tries to please everyone.

A: She's afraid of losing the people around her, and of not being loved. Do you know where that comes from?

N: Other people. She never thought she fit in, that she belonged.

A: And why did she feel that way?

N: Because we were overweight.

A: Let us ask Sophia why she chose that body before she reincarnated, as we choose our own body.

N: For protection.

A: Okay, protection from what?

N: From being hurt.

A: How can an overweight body protect you from being injured?

N: It is a kind of defense.

A: Defense of what?

N: I am not sure.

A: Okay. So, this is something I need to go over with her.

That information provided by Sophia's mother had given me a clue about a past life where feeling vulnerable had originated.

A: What else do you want to tell her before you leave?

N: Don't feel guilt. Put it aside. I love you.

Thus a sad memory, in which Sophia felt guilty for not having called her mother the night she died, was transformed into a positive one. After a few minutes of dialogue between the two of them, that guilty conscience for the suffering she had caused her in life turned into love.

THE SPACE OF 'NO TIME' AND OTHER SPIRITS

Where I use communication in the space of 'no time' the most is in my clients' memories with their loved ones. I also use it when they mention feeling the presence of a spirit nearby.

These may have occurred during their childhood, when they felt someone sitting on their bed while they were sleeping, being touched, or heard someone calling their name. Some people have told me of seeing shadows or feeling a pressure on their body, as if someone was hovering over them.

These are cases in which it is essential to find out what really happened and if, in case it was the presence of a spirit, we will have to find out why it was there and what it wanted to tell us.

It is not uncommon to discover that, in reality, what the person was perceiving was a lost soul in their home and could even be someone who had previously lived and died there.

The Medium Who Did Not Want Her Gift

Sandra has been able to see spirits since she was a child. When she arrived at my door, she knew she possessed a gift, but preferred to ignore it as it caused her fear and nervousness, causing her to block herself out during supernatural experiences.

It did not matter that, several times, I explained to her how this psychic ability could help lost souls. She simply did not want to acknowledge it.

Already in a trance, Sandra went to a memory of when she was a little girl and saw a figure wrapped in fire sitting on her bed. After reviewing this event, she traveled to another one that had taken place about five years before our session, when she had not yet met her current boyfriend.

Antonio: Now, Sandra, I want you to move in time and space in search of another sad event. Five, four, three, two, one. You are already there. Tell me what comes to your mind.

Sandra: "Nothing," she answered in a flat voice.

A: That means no more sad memories. That's good! So, now I'm going to count from five to one and I want you to go to that time during your childhood when you saw a figure on fire sitting in your room. Five, four, three, two, one. You are already there. In that event, is it day or night?

S: At night.

A: What is happening?

S: I am lying in my room. I open my eyes and there is a figure on fire sitting at the foot of my bed.

A: How do you feel there?

S: Scared.

A: And, has that figure done anything to you?

S: No, it just sits there.

A: So, there's no reason to be scared because, if it wanted to do something to you, it would have done it already. The best way to find out what it is doing there is to ask it. Ask that figure who it is and what it is doing there, and it will communicate with you mentally. Let me know how it responds.

S: It doesn't say anything. It has no mouth.

A: Ah, no. It's not going to talk to you, it's going to communicate tele-pathically. What you see is an energy. Tell me what reaches your mind.

S: A demon.

A: All right, then ask that demon what it's there for. What does it say?

S: Nothing.

A: Do you want to lend it your mind and lips so I can talk to it?

S: "No," she answered flatly, shaking her head from side to side.

A: So, what do you want to tell it? Remember, if it were a demon, it would have done something to you by now. Besides, demons don't exist. There are only spirits more advanced than others. Tell it not to scare you like that, not to appear in your bed because you don't understand what it wants.

S: It tells me to take care of myself.

A: You see, do you realize? If it were a demon, it wouldn't ask you to take care of yourself. It looks like it's saying goodbye.

At that instant, Sandra began to breathe faster as several tears began to well up in her eyes.

S: It scares me.

A: Don't be scared. I will explain. Those energies can see your aura. That's why they know you can see them. And, because they know you sense them, they seek you out to communicate. Have any of them ever done anything to you?

S: No.

A: Of course. That spirit told you something nice, to take care of yourself. An evil spirit would not tell you something like that. Ask it who it is and what message it wants to convey to you.

S: "My grandfather," she said as more tears began to fall down her cheeks.

A: Very good, wonderful. Since your grandfather is there, ask him what he wants to tell you, because the communication is open.

S: He tells me that he wanted to meet me.

A: Perfect. Grandfather, thank you for the communication. You know what path your granddaughter will start down and what skill she pos-sesses. What advice do you want to give her today?

Grandfather: Not to trust in everything, but only in her heart; and not to be afraid to listen.

A: Grandfather, can you tell your granddaughter why she should not be afraid to listen?

G: Because they are good energies.

A: Can you tell her what she has to do with her gift of being able to see good energies?

G: Trust.

A: Grandfather, do you know why your granddaughter chose to have this psychic ability in this reincarnation?

G: Because it is strong.

A: Should she start helping others in that way?

G: Yes.

A: Imagine that these lost energies haven't even realized that their body has died. Shouldn't your granddaughter help them then?

G: Yes.

Thus, Sandra's grandfather had appeared before her, when she was just a child, to give her this message. Her initial fear caused her to have a misperception about this presence. Her beliefs had led her to believe that it was a negative energy, like a demon. Once she was able to overcome her fear, Grandpa was able to convey the message and give her the calm she needed.

After this experience, I asked her to go in search of some other past event. So, Sandra began to describe an intense yellow light that would not allow her to open her eyes. The light told her that she had to open her eyes and relax, for it was God who was appearing before her.

A: Since you are spirit, from there, where you are, I want you to imagine that you are coming out of your body. I want you to float to one of the corners of the room and, as you float, see everything that is going on in your room. What is going on? What or who is in your room?

S: There is a lot of light in the whole room, and I see something lying on top of me, but not above me. There is space between us. It is white.

A: Light is always good, and the darker it is the better because it means it is more advanced. Ask that light who it is and why it is there. Tell me whatever comes to your mind.

S: A young boy.

A: Ask that child why he is looking for you.

S: He is lost.

A: Ask that child what happened to him and how his body died.

S: He doesn't tell me anything.

A: Then ask him not to tell you, but to show you. He can put a picture in your mind. Tell him to show you how his body passed away.

S: Asleep.

A: So, he didn't realize it when he died?

S: He did not realize it.

A: Ask him if he knows why the body died.

S: "He was sick," she answered, breathing heavily.

A: Ask him how you can help him.

Sandra was very upset. The communication with this spirit was generating all kinds of emotions in her. Despite my attempts to calm her down so that she could continue the dialogue, she was having a hard time staying calm. Suddenly, she began to cry even more, as it seemed she had already realized who this spirit was.

S: "He's my boyfriend's brother," she said.

A: So, that's why he's looking for you. Calm down. Ask him what he wants to tell your boyfriend. Just repeat back to me what he says. Disconnect the feelings and emotions because they are not yours. How can we help him? Why is he looking for you?

S: "I don't understand," she replied, shaking her head from side to side.

A: You just repeat. Don't try to understand. Do you want me to ask him the questions? What's his name?

S: I don't know.

A: "Brother, you can communicate today," I indicated, touching Sandra's forehead, as if starting a conversation. "Why are you looking for Sandra?"

S: He needs me to help his brother (Sandra's boyfriend) close the chapter of his death.

A: I understand. So, your brother has not closed the chapter on your death.

S: No.

A: How did that body die?

S: From a disease.

A: So, to help your brother close the chapter of your death, what message do you want to convey to him?

S: Not to feel guilty.

A: And why does he feel guilty?

S: Because he thinks that, being his older brother, he could have helped him.

A: That is to say that he does not accept that human beings leave when it is our turn to leave, when we complete our cycle.

S: He does not accept it.

A: In order for him to validate and believe this message, can you tell him something that only you and he knew? Perhaps a word, a memory, or an anecdote.

S: That I am free as a hummingbird.

A: Does he know what that means?

S: Yes.

What had just happened was unbelievable. Five years ago, the spirit of her boyfriend's brother had manifested itself to Sandra to deliver a message. But what was even more incredible was the fact that that message was going to be recovered five years later to be delivered to her brother.

A Spirit at Home

Cristina's childhood and adolescence had been quite complicated. Her father abandoned her and her mother and, in turn, her mother did not pay attention to her. As a result, she grew up with her grandmother, but when she was a teenager, she had to be placed in a nursing home. Because of all this, she had felt a lot of accumulated sadness since she was just a child.

Already in a trance, Cristina turned to a memory of her adolescence, when she was at home doing her chores.

Antonio: Five, four, three, two, one. You're already there.

Cristina: I'm at home cleaning the apartment. They've gone shopping.

A: So, what's going on?

C: A hand touched me. Big! It touched my left arm. It feels very cold.

A: So, how do you feel?

C: Very scared.

A: You are spirit and there are no limits of time or space. You can get out of your body and look at that scene from above. Look at the room from above. It's you cleaning the floor and who else?

C: A big man. He has no face.

A: Is it like a shadow?

C: His hand is the one I feel. His hand is there.

A: He grabs you with his hand. Is he behind you?

C: Yes.

A: Do you want to offer him your mind and lips to communicate with me?

C: Okay.

A: All right, I'm going to count from three to one. When I get to one, you're going to lend him your mind and lips to communicate with me. Three, two, one. Switch. Brother, good evening, can you tell me who you are?

Lost Soul: I live here!

A: So, tell me. When you had a body, were you a man or a woman?

LS: Male.

A: What was your name? What did they call you?

LS: I don't remember.

A: And, brother, how did your body die?

LS: Sick.

A: What happened to you, what illness did you have?

LS: Lungs.

A: And, tell me why you are bothering Cristina.

LS: She is alone.

A: Yes, she is alone, but she is just a girl cleaning.

LS: She is a very sad child.

A: Yes, I know. Can you see that from where you are?

LS: Yes.

A: So, she's sad and you grab her arm and scare her, what do you think?

LS: I just wanted to help.

A: Oh, I understand. And, I'll ask you a question, have you been attached to her since that day or are you at home? Are you with her?

LS: "I'm with her," he said, referring to him being attached to her energetic body.

A: I know you wanted to help her because she was very sad, but why did you attach to her?

LS: "Because she is alone, very alone," he answered with tears in his eyes.

A: Are there any symptoms that you have caused her? She has pain in her arm and back, did you cause that?

LS: Yes.

A: Is that what you felt when you died of your lungs?

LS: Yes.

A: Are you the one blocking it?

LS: No.

A: She doesn't remember things from her childhood. Are you the one blocking her?

LS: No. There is someone else.

A: Thank you for letting me know. Another question, do you have anything to do with the noises she hears in her house?

LS: No, there is someone else.

A: All right, brother. I know you attached to her because she was sad and lonely, but it's time we left her because your good intentions are causing her physical discomfort. Would you like to go to the light today?

LS: I was waiting for you.

This was one of the first times a spirit told me that they were waiting to talk to me in a session.

A: Were you waiting for me?

LS: I was waiting for you.

A: Do you know about me?

LS: Yes.

A: What do you know about me?

LS: You are a guide.

A: What else can you tell me? Do you know what my mission is?

LS: To help. I was waiting for you.

A: Okay, then, do you want to apologize to Cristina for those symptoms that you unintentionally provoked? Because I know you meant well.

LS: Yes.

A: Please tell her. She is listening to you.

LS: Forgive me. I didn't mean to scare you. I was in the dark, just like you.

A: All right, we are going to talk to Cristina now. Three, two, one. Switch. Cristina, did you realize that we have a spiritual brother, a man who died in that house who wanted to help you?

C: Yes.

A: His good intentions caused you those symptoms, which he felt when his body died. Do you want to forgive him today?

C: "Yes," she replied with tears running down her cheeks.

This is how the spirits of both worked out forgiveness. I asked the man to leave Christina's body, and then leave for the light, taking the symptoms and his energy with him.

The other spirit the man referred to was that of Cristina's grandmother. This one was not attached to her, but was there to give her a message.

PAST LIVES

As I explained pages ago, it is fundamental to understand that the past does not exist and that everything happens in the now. Referring to past lives will basically help us to understand what the linear progression is during the navigation of events in a hypnosis session.

Understanding what a past life is and considering this concept during the session is an elemental part of the therapy approach. And, not only for our client, but also for the lost soul that may be attached to him/her.

Every therapist, whether they like it or not, will sooner or later find themselves navigating a client's past life. This will be the result of working with the symptoms that the person brings to the meeting. It is important to know that these physical and/or psychological manifestations that have no medical explanation could have originated in intrauterine life, early childhood, or adulthood, but also during a past life.

Trauma means that there is an unresolved issue, something that our spirit could not process correctly on a physical, emotional, and mental level, leading to soul entrapment and fragmentation. It does not matter if the event occurred 15 or 1,000 years ago in another body.

How is this possible? It is possible because, for the soul, time does not exist and because part of it is imprisoned in the traumatic experience that occurred 1,000 years ago, causing it to be relived again and again until today.

So, could we say that the unexplainable illnesses we suffer today may come from experiences in other bodies, generally the ones related to the agony of the body itself? Yes, the trauma is essentially generated when the spirit does not process death correctly.

What is the Point of Navigating a Past Life?

I have seen many hypnotists, hypnotherapists and regressionists lose their therapeutic focus and line of work by trying to get too many details about that past life that their client or patient comes to. Many become obsessed with minutiae that really have no therapeutic value.

For example, if that past life was in the Inca Empire, surely, some will focus on asking questions about Incan constructions, the social organization of the empire, their astronomical knowledge, or how they buried their dead. From a therapeutic point of view, of what use would this information be to my client? Very little, if anything.

Navigating a past life can inform us about the root cause of symptoms and traumas, as well as help us understand other aspects of a person's current reincarnation:

- Behavioral patterns brought into the current life.
- Relationships with other people and problems with them.
- Origin of fears and phobias.
- Understanding why they face the same lesson in this life.
- Lessons to be learned, as well as whether the objectives planned for that reincarnation were achieved.

Each past life has a story that must be discovered by the therapist. This will help our client to understand the situations he/she is currently facing. It is similar to looking for the missing pieces of a puzzle, which requires a lot of patience and attention to detail.

Past Life Evaluation

A vital part of navigating a past life is to find out how that body died. As I have said before, many of the unexplained symptoms we experience now may be related to how our body died in another life.

It is also important to decipher what else was happening during the last minutes of that reincarnation: the individuals present, what the person was thinking, their state of mind, if they were conscious at the moment of departure, if they were ready to die or not, among other things. Being aware of this will help us to know if there was an entrapment or fragmentation of the soul.

In the next chapter, we will understand more about this subject, but for now, it is necessary to understand that every person must be guided through the moment of death of the body, no matter how traumatic it may have been. This is part of our work and what will help to end entrapment.

The navigation and understanding of past lives applies to both our clients (reincarnated spirits) and the lost souls that may be attached to them. My goal is for that person's soul to understand for themselves what is going on, while disconnecting them from that life and that body by saying "with the death of that body, that life is over forever and nothing you experienced will affect you negatively."

In uttering these words, my intention is to end soul entrapment, if any. I then ask the following questions by way of self-evaluation:

1. What do you think you had to learn in that life?

2. Do you believe that you passed that lesson?

3. If the answer to the above question is no, then I ask: what do you still need to learn?

4. Why do you think you didn't pass that lesson?

5. Based on that life experience and since you know what they are facing now, what advice can you give to (my client's name)?

6. Do you feel like you are repeating the same lesson in (my client's name)'s life?

7. How many lifetimes have you spent learning that lesson?

8. How many more are you willing to use to learn it?

Referring to the person they were in that past life and who they are in the current one as if they were different people makes the communication flow better and my client does not get confused. The spirit is the same, but part of it is out of the body that just died and the other is with my client in my office. The one that is out of the body has a better understanding because it is in a subtle dimension, where it can get more and better information about the plan and goals it had set for itself, both in that life and in the current one.

If we look at this scenario, what is actually happening is that spirit is giving advice to itself based on my questions. As other therapists would say, the client is communicating with their 'Higher Self', the area of their soul connected to the spiritual world that has all the information they need. It is this knowledge that will help them make the changes they need to make in the current life to overcome their lessons.

If the life that has just ended is that of a lost soul attached to our client, the end is the same. I will help them find out what they should have learned and why they got trapped or decided not to go to the light.

There will be times when we will find out that the spirit did not go to the light out of a desire for revenge towards those who killed them or because of a promise they made to a loved one: "I will never leave you" or "I will always be with you."

I am one of those hypnotherapists who believe that one should not visit past lives out of curiosity. Going through a past reincarnation should always have a therapeutic focus, such as helping to achieve a greater understanding of who we are and what we are here for.

WHY DOES A LOST SOUL ATTACH?

There are several reasons that can lead a lost soul to attach to our vibratory field, since each one has its own history and reason for having decided to stay in this plane.

The list I will provide is based solely on my own experiences with my clients. There may be many more.

- **Unfinished Business**

One of the greatest difficulties the soul has when leaving the body that has just died is the feeling of still having tasks to complete. For example, it happens when the individual dies young with a promising future, soon after having started a life as a couple, having young children, or not having been able to meet their grandchildren.

More than once, I have had to assist lost souls who had stayed in the house where they lived. They did not want to leave because they did not accept that the new tenants would enjoy what they had built with so much effort.

- **Conflict with the Victim**

Let us remember that, for the spirit, time does not exist. If it had some conflict in a past life or in the present one with someone, it is very likely that it has attached itself to them in search of revenge, trying to cause them all kinds of problems. It does not matter that the spirit, which is the victim of this spiritual attachment, has a different body now. The spirit of the victim is still the same and because of its unique vibrational frequency, the vengeful spirit will find it.

One case I remember was that of a man whose wife was unfaithful with his best friend and between the two of them they had murdered him to keep his property. Out of rage and seeking revenge, this soul did not want to leave.

- **Sent by Someone Else**

This is the case of spirits who lend themselves to collaborate in works of witchcraft. The supposed witches offer them something in exchange for their participation, but the reality is that, by lending themselves to this, they are becoming a victim in turn.

- **Opportunism**

There will also be spirits who have no unfinished business or conflict with their victim, and who did not even know them when they had a body. They simply saw the opportunity and attached themselves to them.

In the cases I have witnessed, these attachments took place at wakes, cemeteries, hospitals, and accident scenes.

- **Habits and Addictions of its Victim**

This is the soul that wants to continue experiencing its habits and addictions through the body of its victim.

If the victim is addicted to drugs, then it is very likely that he or she has attached to it in order to continue experiencing the effects that the substance produced. The same applies to any other type of addiction or habit.

I remember one of the cases that a colleague of mine had, in which the spirit attached to her client had been a prostitute in her last life and made her victim behave that way when there was a man she liked.

These lost souls not only play a passive role, for example, waiting for the person to use the drug, but will incite them to do so, making them feel their own urges and desires.

- **Waiting for a Loved One**

There is always the case of the wife or husband who has to leave and who, not wanting to leave his or her partner alone, decides to stay and adhere to him or her, waiting for the moment when it will be his or her turn to leave as well.

As I have mentioned before, even if the intention is good, every time a lost soul attaches itself to the aura of its victim, the victim will experience all kinds of symptoms and emotions that the parasitic energy transmits to it.

On several occasions, I have asked a client what was going on in their life or around them when the symptom that afflicted them began. To my surprise, their response has been, "At the time of death of my grandmother, grandfather, father, mother, an uncle, a friend, etc". That physical or psychological manifestation they felt was the same as this loved one felt before they died. The soul of the loved one had attached itself to them after their death.

- **Waiting to Give a Message**

We were able to appreciate this situation in the session of María—in "César's Message"—to whom César had attached himself in order to contact her aunt and ask for her forgiveness.

Spirits will try to communicate to their loved ones what they could not tell them before or while their body was dying. This applies not only to those lost souls who are trapped, but also to spirits who wish to dialogue before leaving for the light or who come from the light to deliver a message.

In these cases, we must proceed with care, verifying that they are who they say they are.

- **To Ask for Forgiveness**

Something I learned from hypnotherapist José Luis Cabouli is the concept that every victim has been an aggressor before. If we look at it from the point of view of karma, later on, we will experience what we made others feel in the same or greater intensity.

If we look at it from the point of view of reincarnation, we will all play different roles. Sometimes we will be heroes, sometimes villains and sometimes observers. In other words, sooner or later we will be victims and aggressors as well.

On the other hand, if we look at it from the point of view of soul entrapment, an aggressor may realize or regret what they did while their body is dying or once they leave it and have understanding of the magnitude of what they did, feeling guilty and perhaps saying "I don't deserve God's forgiveness" or "I will never forgive myself."

At that moment, the aggressor will become a victim and their soul may become trapped or, if they reincarnate, they may begin to sabotage themselves because they feel they do not deserve forgiveness. Let us remember that, for the spirit, time has not passed, and it still remembers what it did in its life as the aggressor.

The Owner of the Wake

We return to the session of María, a woman from Central America who had gone through many sad and traumatic situations through her mother. Recall that the first spirit to appear that day was that of César, who had a message for the aunt. Before going to the light, I asked for his help in removing the symptoms he had provoked in her.

Antonio: César, as you can see, María has already forgiven you. Now, may I ask you a great favor, brother?

César: Yes, tell me.

A: Can you help me remove all that energy that has caused problems for María with the right side of her face, right arm, foot, and chest? Can you help me?

C: It's not just me. There is one other person (spirit) too.

A: Okay, we will talk to that person in a moment.

C: I would be happy to help you.

A: Perfect, then I ask you to wait there for a moment while we talk to this other person. Where is the person located?

C: "Always on the right foot," he said, raising his hand and pointing to it with his index finger.

A: "Okay, I am going to take that energy and bring it to your mind so that it can express itself. Brother, you can communicate now," I said, touching María's forehead, "How long have you been with María?"

Lost Soul: A long, long time ago.

A: When you had a body, were you a man or a woman?

LS: I was a woman.

A: And what was your name?

LS: I don't remember.

A: Can I give you a name for the time being?

LS: "No!" she answered emphatically.

A: You are unique, aren't you?

LS: Yes!

A: No problem, why are you with María?

LS: I've always been in her.

A: Why, what were you looking for from her?

LS: I possessed her.

A: Well, we know that there is no such thing as possession. What you have done is attach to her energy.

LS: "Yes," she nodded in agreement.

A: And that's where you are living.

LS: Yes, and I want to continue living here.

A: It's good that we have that concept clear. As for continuing to live there, let's see how I can help you. Where was it that you met María? When did you become attached to her body?

LS: At a wake.

A: At whose wake?

LS: "Mine," she replied, touching her chest.

A: So she goes as a good person to your wake to mourn your departure and you take advantage of that and attach to her.

LS: Yes.

A: So, people will think it's better not to go to wakes because the dead person might attach to them. That's not right, is it?

LS: "No," she said, shaking her head from side to side, "I want to stay there."

A: Well, let's talk about it. You have clung to María, but this is not your body. That means you are not in the light and that is why you have clung to this physical plane. Why could you not go to the light? Did you have some unfinished business?

LS: Yes, with my mom.

A: What did your mother do to you?

LS: She's a bad mom.

A: Do you remember what she was called?

LS: Juana.

A: What did your mother do to you? Maybe she has already passed to the other plane too.

LS: Yes.

A: What did your mother do to you?

LS: "She sold me," she answered very sadly.

A: How old were you when your body died?

LS: Sixteen years.

A: Were you unhappy since your mom sold you?

LS: Yes.

A: You know we are evolving spirits. Your mom may have acquired a debt for what she did, which she will have to pay off in another life. We are all in an evolutionary process. There is no right or wrong and, therefore, we should not judge.

LS: "I want to open my eyes and I can't!" she said, interrupting me and making gestures with her hands, "I want to see my mom and I can't!"

A: You can't because, for one thing, your mother is no longer on this plane and, for another, this is not your body.

LS: I want to tell her that I forgive her.

A: That's right! She is spirit and, from the light, she will hear you. What do you want to tell her?

LS: That I forgive her.

A: Then, I am going to put my hand on your chest and you will put there all that resentment that you no longer need. You will forgive your mother. Let me know when you have put all those unnecessary negative feelings that do not allow you to evolve. You tell me and I will take them away.

LS: Yes, I want to forgive my mom.

A: All right! I'll take them, I'll take them, they're gone! What do you want to put in the place where all of them were?

LS: Much peace!

A: A lot of peace, a lot of light and forgiveness. Perfect! Now, I ask you, what did you consciously or unconsciously provoke in María? Any symptoms?

LS: Yes, headache.

A: The one on the side here? I asked, pointing to the right side of her head.

LS: A lot of pain.

A: Can you help me remove it? She doesn't need it anymore.

LS: "I want to stay here," she said with a frown.

A: Wait, let me explain something to you. You are in the shadow because you have not gone into the light. You have told me that you want to go out and continue your evolution, that you want María to forgive you. Sister, you have to get out of there, go to the light and return to this world in another body. Surely there is a pending matter with your mother that needs to be settled, but until you go to the light, there will be no evolution. Shall we go to the light?

LS: "Yes," she replied with a gesture of resignation.

A: Perfect! Let me talk to María for a moment. María, did you listen to the spiritual sister you have there with you? She was lost, confused, did we forgive her for that? This all works on the basis of forgiveness.

María: Yes.

A: Sister, María has already forgiven you. Before you go into the light, can you help me remove all those problems you have caused her?

Thus, having elaborated forgiveness, the spirit of the young woman departed into the light, withdrawing all the symptoms she had caused, which in reality belonged to her.

The Spirit of a Rapist

As you have been able to appreciate, María's session was intense and complex. We had already communicated with César and the spirit of the young woman who attached to her at her wake, and were able to help both of them, when a third spirit appeared. Now, it was Raúl's turn, who had also manifested at the beginning of the session.

Antonio: César, thank you for letting me know that the young lady was there. Now, can you help us remove María's other symptoms?

César: "I'm getting out of here. I'm going to leave your niece alone," he said to María's aunt.

A: Before you go, can you see if everything is okay with the swelling she feels in her chest? Was it caused by you?

C: "That has nothing to do with us," he replied, shaking his head from side to side.

A: But can you help me take it away??

C: That belongs to her mother. No, no, no, no, that belongs to her mother. Leave me alone. Please, that's not mine. I just take away the pain I caused her.

A: "All right, let's go out this way," I indicated by touching the top of his head, "We thank you for your help, may the peace of the universe be with you. Collect all your energy and come out."

A few seconds later, I returned to dialogue with María to decipher the origin of the swelling in her chest, which she described as a protruding bone.

A: "María, César is out. Please cover your whole body with light. You are spirit and I want you to analyze your body from where you are. Look at your body spiritually and tell me what you see here," I said, touching her chest.

María: A bone.

A: What's the deal with that bone?

M: "I feel something horrible, very ugly," she answered trembling.

A: Be calm, we're going to take that feeling and I'm going to take it into your mind. Let it express itself. Brother, you can communicate now. How long have you been with María?

Lost Soul: "Many years!" he answered in a very deep voice, "And I won't leave her alone!"

A: "Okay, no problem. I'm not telling you anything. Tell me, in your past life were you a man or a woman? You spoke to me with that deep voice" I said, imitating him. "It seems you were a man, right?"

LS: I don't remember.

A: Well, it doesn't matter. Now, you're spirit, what are you doing with her?

LS: Not leaving her alone.

A: Did you know her?

LS: I don't remember.

A: Did you cause something for her voluntarily or involuntarily?

LS: Yes.

A: The pain here? I asked pointing to his chest.

LS: Yes

A: Do you regret having caused that?

LS: No.

A: So, tell me why you provoked it.

LS: I hate her mom!

A: Tell me who you are. Why do you hate her?

LS: She hurt me a lot.

A: Let's see, there's something I want to understand here because it seems that María also had a problem with her mom.

LS: She knew me, María. She knows who I am.

A: May I ask her?

LS: No, she was very young.

A: So you were the mother's partner?

LS: Yes.

A: So, what happened to you, how did you pass to the spiritual plane?

LS: His mom forced me, she forced me!

A: Forced you to what?

LS: "I didn't want to. I told her no," he said with tears in his eyes.

A: Not what?

LS: I... I told her mother that I didn't want to rape her.

A: Ah, you were the one who raped her.

LS: "I didn't want to, I didn't want to!" she uttered as she cried desperately. "I was too much of a child."

A: Brother, how old were you when that happened?

LS: Twenty-four years. I didn't want to. She forced me.

A: What power did she have over you?

LS: "I don't know, she's bad!" he said, moving his whole body.

A: Do you regret that? Do you want María to forgive you?

LS: Yes, she has suffered a lot because of that.

A: "Let me talk to her for a moment, please. María," I called out to her, touching her forehead, "Have you seen that we have an attached brother over there who is the one who did something to you when you were a child?"

M: "I know," she replied in a soft, calm voice.

A: Do you realize that he is repentant? Do you forgive him for that ignorance? Because he didn't know what he was doing.

M: I don't know what's wrong with me, but I can't. I can't forgive him. I can't forgive him.

A: We evolve in the spiritual world through forgiveness.

M: "Brother, I can't," she said shaking her head.

Let us remember the concept I spoke of above, that every victim has been an aggressor before. Since María could not forgive, it only remained for her to find out if they had met in a past life, where there was outstand-ing karma, or if María had done the same.

A: María, I'm going to count to three and I want you to go to a life where you knew him. Let's see if you two knew each other before. Three, two, one. Place yourself in that life. Tell me if you knew him before.

M: "His name is Raúl," she recalled admiringly. "Yes, his name is Raúl."

This was the same name that had appeared at the beginning of the ses-sion.

A: Did you know him in that life?

M: Yes.

A: And did you do something to him?

S: Yes.

A: What did you do to him?

M: I cheated on him.

A: What kind of cheating?

M: "I left with someone else," she answered with a mocking laugh.

We had found the unfinished business between them. What Raúl's lost soul needed to go to the light was María forgiveness.

Realizing that in a past life she had been the victimizer, María was able to forgive Raúl. Once the two had forgiven each other, Raúl departed into the light, taking with him the symptoms he had caused María.

A Vengeful Sexual Predator

When explaining, during the Introspective Hypnosis course, the tech-niques used in a session, how psychosomatic symptoms usually manifest themselves, and, while the participants are practicing the techniques on themselves, it is normal that certain symptoms are activated in them or that they begin to understand where the discomfort and torments they suffer come from. Obviously, I am referring to those ailments that have no medical or logical explanation.

That was the case of Bianca, who began to experience more intensely the symptoms she had been having since she was a child and for which the doctors had not found an origin.

At 48 years old, Bianca suffered from headaches and neck pain. From time to time, she felt burning in her kidneys and that her hands burned when she woke up in the morning. She also mentioned feeling a great sadness and that, despite being surrounded by people, she felt very lonely.

Once the session started, I was able to detect that Bianca was not visual, that is, she could not see images of the events she visited while in trance, but she could feel in her body everything that was happening at that moment.

Antonio: I am going to count from five to one and, while I count, I want you to look for a sad memory, one that has frustrated you or made you feel bad. Five, four, three, two, one. You're already there. Let yourself remember. Is it day or night?

Bianca: I don't know.

A: Okay, so you feel. What are you feeling there?

B: I can feel my heart beating very hard.

A: That's it! Feel that, feel it even more, what else is going on?

B: "Nothing, my heart just stopped," she said, putting her hand on her chest, a sign that gave me a hint of what was to come next.

A: Now, I want you to feel that more intensely. That thing you're feeling in your heart, does it feel like what's happening to your heart?

B: "I don't feel it as intense now, but I can feel it in my throat," she explained, bringing her hand to her neck.

A: And, if you knew, what's happening to the heart?

B: I can't get enough air.

A: And, if you knew, where are you while your heart is beating and you can't catch your breath?

B: I don't know. I'm feeling emotional and I don't know why.

A: And, where are you while you're feeling all that?

B: "I don't know, but I can't get enough air," she said, touching her throat and bursting into tears. "I'm sad, I don't know what's going on. I don't know what's going on, I feel so sad!"

I spent a few more minutes trying to define if what I was experiencing was a past life or a lost soul attached to her. Bianca didn't understand what was happening, but she was definitely feeling it all in her body: the pain in her chest, the shortness of breath, and a great sadness.

I tried to communicate with a possible lost soul that is causing these symptoms, but got no response. For this reason, I continued to navigate that experience, assuming that it was a past life.

A: What else is going on?

B: I feel like I'm lying with a rock on my chest.

A: That's it! Feel that pressure, that you can't breathe.

B: I feel that I am alone. There is no one there. I don't know if it's day or night.

A: I'm going to count from three to one and I want you to go to the moment when this experience begins. Three, two, one. If you knew, how would you say this experience begins?

B: I feel a discomfort in my stomach, as if I am sick, and it goes up to my throat.

A: What is happening to your stomach?

B: I can't see anything. I can only feel what is happening.

A: I don't want you to see, I want you to feel. Tell me if you are a man or a woman there.

B: "I feel that I am a woman and I feel it in my stomach," she said, making gestures of discomfort. "I'm lying on a bed and I feel like I have to vomit. I feel nauseous. Now I'm getting a headache. I'm alone, lying there and sick."

A: So far, what has been the most difficult moment of this experience?

B: Feeling sad.

A: What are your physical reactions?

B: "I feel so bad," she answered, breaking into tears once again. "I don't know why I'm sad. I think it's because I'm lonely."

A: And, as you feel bad and lonely, what are your emotional reactions?

B: I have no one. I feel like I am alone and sick in a big house. I have no one.

A: What are your mental reactions while you are sick and alone?

B: I don't want to be alone. Where is everybody?

A: Now, I want you to see how all this is hurting your life as Bianca. What happens when you feel bad and alone?

B: I feel it in my heart.

A: What does that stop you from doing?

B: Make contact because I am afraid of being rejected.

A: Now, I'm going to count from three to one and I want you to go to the beginning of this experience, to the moment when all this begins, to see why you are alone. Allow your body to feel everything it needs to feel. Three, two, one. You are already there. What is happening?

B: I am very sad!

A: And, if you knew, why would you say you were sad?

B: "I can feel it in my heart," she replied, putting both hands to her chest and throat.

A: and what is causing that sadness?

B: "I can't talk," she said, clutching her throat. "My chest and throat hurt. Oh, my God!"

I spent a few more minutes trying to decipher the story behind this supposed past life, although, at times, it felt like we were walking in circles around the same ailments.

A: I want you to see why you are alone. Where is everyone?

B: I don't know. Everyone is busy.

A: Who are they?

B: My mom is busy.

A: And how old are you there?

B: Seven.

A: What do people call you?

B: "Bianca," she answered touching her eyelids, while crying with a more childish attitude.

A: Now, I'm going to count from three to one and I want you to go back to when all this started, to when you felt sad and lonely. Three, two, one. You are already there. If you knew, where would you say you are now?

B: I feel pressure in my chest. I don't know where I am. I feel energy in my feet and pressure in my chest.

A: There, where you are, do you have the body of a man or a woman?

B: I think I am a woman.

A: What is happening to your body?

B: I need air. I can't breathe. I'm outside, it feels like I'm looking out to sea. I need air and I'm so sad. My God, I feel so sad, but I don't know why. I need air... my chest!

A: What else is going on?

B: "I feel energy in my feet, my legs... I need air!" she cried desperately, "I don't know what's happening to me. My head hurts from lack of oxygen."

A: What else is going on?

B: My chest feels like it's about to explode. I am a woman and I am no longer standing. I'm lying on the floor.

Bianca had reached the moment of death of that body. Now, she had to find out what that energy was that she had mentioned a few times and the cause of her death. For this, I needed her to go back a bit in that life.

A: I need you to go back before all this started. Three, two, one. What's going on?

B: I feel something in my stomach. It feels like I'm in a classroom. I am a teacher. I'm sitting and I feel something in my stomach. I have black hair. That's all I see.

A: And, what are you feeling in your stomach?

B: I feel like something is about to happen, something difficult.

A: Move to the moment something happens. Three, two, one. You're already there. What's happening now?

B: I don't have enough air and I feel pressure in my chest. I feel anxious about something I can't see but I know it's there—it's an energy! I'm so scared I don't want to turn around.

A: Continue...

B: "I've turned to face something I can't see," she said, breathing quickly and crying, "but it's there. I don't know what it is. I feel like I can't breathe. I have tension all over my body and a lot of fear. I don't know what's happening!"

A: Up to this point, what has been the most difficult moment?

B: What I can't see, but I can feel. I can feel it, but I don't know where it is or what it is.

A: And what are your physical reactions?

B: The back of my head hurts.

A: And what are your emotional reactions?

B: I want him to leave.

A: And, when you have a headache and you want it to go away, what are your mental reactions?

B: Try to make it stop.

A: Now, I want you to see how all this affects your life as Bianca. When the back of your head hurts, when you want it to stop, what does it make you do?

B: Hide.

A: And, hiding, what's stopping you from doing that?

B: I don't want to feel anything, but I feel it.

A: What happens next?

B: I feel it in my feet and back. I feel the energy going up into my knees and legs. It keeps going up. I feel my heart pounding.

A: Go ahead and see what happens.

B: I feel it in my chest. It's a pressure that won't go away, but there's no one there.

By this time, I had been able to decipher that it was this energy that was tormenting her and causing her to suffer from these symptoms. Although Bianca could not understand what was happening, I could feel what was going to happen next. So, I moved her to the last moment of that life to understand how that body was dying.

A: Fast forward to the last moment of that life.

B: "I feel something coming in through my back. Now, it's in my body and I feel it in my stomach. I am lying down. It makes me breathe fast and my feet feel cold. I feel a weight on my shoulders pulling me down and it hurts," she recounted through tears. "I am so sad. I feel... oh my God! My neck and my legs. I can't breathe. My throat. I have no air. I feel a pressure in my chest... oh, my God! I feel an intense pressure in my chest that is taking my energy. It's getting into me. It is very intense."

This is how that woman's body died in that life, feeling everything provoked by that energy: panic, pain, shortness of breath, submerged in tears. and fear.

I'm not saying that a lost soul has the power to kill someone, but, apparently, what it made her feel caused her to panic so much that she became short of breath until she felt a pressure in her chest—possibly a heart attack—causing her to die.

A: I want you to move to the moment when you get out of the body, becoming aware that, with the death of that body, that experience is over forever and none of it belongs to you anymore. Now that you are out of the body, you can see who did this to you. What went into your back? Look at your body down there. What's going on?

B: I can't see it, but I can feel it. I can feel her pain. She suffered a lot.

A: Feel that energy. What is that energy that did this to you?

B: I don't know.

A: I want to talk to that energy that did this to that woman. Lend her your mind and lips. Three, two, one. Thank you for the communication. Please, can you let me know who you are?

Lost Soul: "No," they replied in a curt tone.

A: No problem. Tell me why you did that to that woman, why are you so upset with her?

LS: "I don't want it," they said, changing their voice.

A: Do you have any unfinished business with her, do you know her?

LS: I think so.

A: What did she do to you that bothered you so much?

LS: I hate her.

A: Why, what has she done to you? I'm not here to judge you, I just want to help you.

LS: My chest hurts.

A: Did she do something to your chest?

LS: I think so.

A: When you had a body, were you a man or a woman?

LS: I was a man.

A: Let's remember how your body died to have a better understanding. I will count from three to one and you will go to the last moment you had a body. One, two, three. You're already there. What's going on? How does your body die?

LS: With a knife. Oh, my chest hurts!

A: Is the person holding the knife a man or a woman?

LS: A woman.

A: Why is she stabbing you?

LS: Because I touched her improperly.

A: You touched her inappropriately and now she's going to kill you.

LS: I think she already did.

A: Now, I want you to wait there for a moment and let me and her work on this. I want to see what responsibility she has in this, do you think?

LS: Okay.

A: Now, I am talking to the woman who died because of this lost soul. He says you killed him because he touched you wrongly. Do you remember that life?

Bianca: No.

A: I'll count from three to one and I want you to look up the life in which they met. Three, two, one. You're already there. What's going on?

B: I am a girl. I'm wearing a skirt and I'm walking down the street. I am beautiful and I have a purse. It's not dark yet. There is a man in the alley calling me. He seems to want something from me. He looks strange, but he wants something from me. I don't know him. This doesn't look good. He wants me to come closer and starts touching me inappropriately. I have a small knife in my purse and I try to keep him away with it, but he laughs at me. He is pulling me to come closer, but I don't want to, so I use the dagger. I think I've hurt him.

A: Where?

B: In the arm. I don't know what happened. He's pulling my clothes and I use the knife and stab him in the chest. I run away.

A: Perfect, let me talk to that spirit again. Brother, we are understanding what happened. You understand what has happened, right? My question is who started this.

LS: She started it.

A: What do you mean she started it? She was walking and you called out to her. You asked her to come closer and you started touching her inappropriately. Who started all this?

LS: "She with her skirt," he replied, referring to the way she was dressed.

A: "So, what you're saying is that everyone who wears a skirt deserves to be touched inappropriately, right? The truth is that you decided to do it and you had no right. You did something wrong and she reacted and killed you. Was it your intention to kill him?" I asked, turning to the woman.

B: No.

A: You see? She was just defending herself. Wouldn't you do the same thing in her place? So why are you doing that to her in the life she was a teacher in and in this life? When is this going to end? You're trapped and you can't go into the light. You're making her feel things, you're making her uncomfortable, when is this going to end? Why don't we end this today?

LS: "No!" he said with a more serious face.

A: No? Let's show you how this works. I'm talking to the soul of that woman, the teacher, who is also Bianca's soul. Would you like to apologize to this man for killing him, even though you didn't mean to?

B: Yes. I didn't even know I had killed him.

A: Then apologize from the bottom of your heart.

B: I didn't mean to kill you. I didn't know I had killed you so I apologize.

A: Now, give him his energy. The energy that stayed when you killed him.

B: I give you back your energy.

A: Now, do you want to apologize to her for touching her inappropriately?

LS: I like it.

A: And what does that have to do with it? When I go to the park I see beautiful flowers and that doesn't mean I can touch them or pluck them. When you see something beautiful, you should admire that beauty.

LS: I am scared.

A: Scared of what?

LS: I want to stay with her.

A: And what would you gain from that? Nothing, right? You are there, delaying your evolution, accumulating karma for no reason because you killed her in the teacher's life. You are causing discomfort in her present body, and what are you accomplishing? Nothing. She already apologized for killing you, don't you want to apologize now?

LS: Actually, I like her a lot. I like being with her.

A: Do you want to apologize to her?

LS: Okay.

That was how they both forgave each other. The man's lost soul agreed to leave Bianca's vibratory field, taking with him all the symptoms he was causing her. A few minutes later, the session ended successfully. Coming out of the trance, Bianca could not believe what she had experienced. "I had never cried so much," she told me.

The navigation of this session was a bit confusing at first as Bianca began experiencing the symptoms caused by the man's lost soul as soon as she entered trance. As she followed those discomforts, she came to a time in this life when she was a child and experienced them as well. Then, when I asked her to go to the moment when all this started, she came to the life of the teacher, who died because of what the lost soul made her feel.

So how could all this be possible? Let us remember that the soul understands neither time nor space. Bianca's soul went to all the events where she had suffered these symptoms, including those experienced in the teacher's life. For the soul, everything happens now and, from that expanded state of consciousness, it can connect all the dots at once and jump from reincarnation to reincarnation.

Some may wonder how it is possible to have a soul lost in a past life and have it attached to us in this one as well. The explanation is the same. For the soul, there is neither time nor geography. They can find us through the unique frequency that our energy emits.

This was not the first, nor the last time that I have had to help a lost soul that has followed my client's soul from life to life, attaching to their vibratory field. Therefore, it is essential to help both souls to settle the issues they have pending, so they can continue with their evolution, guiding them to work on forgiveness and to get out of the role of victim in which they find themselves because the only thing this generates is the entrapment of their soul.

HOW TO FIND PARASITIC SPIRITS?

We have seen how to work with the spirits of the loved ones of those who come to a hypnosis session. These spirits that I mentioned in the previous section are not attached to the person's energy field. Simply put, during the trance, I take the opportunity to communicate with them through a memory to the one who was my client during the hypnotic regression.

It is possible that, at the time of dialoguing with these spirits, we may be surprised to find that in reality they had not gone to the light for different reasons, even that they had not become aware that their body was already dead. In this case, it would be necessary to understand why they did not see the light, assist them to work on their pending issues and help them in their process.

But how to detect those who are attached to the person's aura? I think it would be impossible to make a manual on how to detect this type of lost souls since we are dealing with something that we cannot see—although we can perceive them—and that has a consciousness and intelligence of its own.

What I can mention are some of the most common ways in which I have been able to detect them, although each session is unique, each person is unique and, therefore, each lost soul is unique.

During a hypnosis session, it is rare that a spirit will willingly give us the information we need: "Wait a minute, now it's my turn to speak.

My name is Joe and I am attached to your client's abdomen. I'm the one causing the pain in that area. By the way, I died a traumatic death. I'm lost and I need you to help me go to the light." How easy it would be if it happened that way. But, usually:

- They do not want to be detected.
- They will not always give us their name.
- We will have to deduce in which area they are attached, following the client's symptoms.
- Many times, they have no idea of the symptoms they cause.
- They may not know they are lost.
- They may not have realized that their body has died.
- There will be times when they won't even want to talk to us.
- Not all of them are motivated to go into the light.

If all of the above is true, then how are we supposed to detect them in order to work with them? While working with our clients, there will be certain episodes that will make us suspect that something is going on, that something does not make sense. It is at that moment that we will cast a kind of fishing rod to see if the fish (parasitic spirit) bites, even though we might not find anything.

It is essential that we are connected and attentive to everything our clients say and do during the trance state, because in an expression, a mark that appears on the skin or a date out of range will be giving us the clue we need to detect them.

We must be alert to the phrases that the person says even from the moment of the hypnotic induction. More than once it has happened to me that, while I am initiating the induction process, my client has said something like, "I don't want to be here," "I want to leave," or "I don't know what I am doing here." Faced with these expressions, I had to ask who was saying that, where he/she would like to be and in which place he/she does not want to be.

What was happening is that the lost soul had already started to manifest and talk to me. That is why our five senses must be at 100% during the whole session.

From the moment we meet our clients and have the first interview with them, we must pay attention to their stories, feelings, and requirements. Thus, it will be easier for us to pick up those phrases that do not make sense and that we feel come from another life or that seem to be said by an entity. They may even appear before the client enters a trance. Detecting them during the interview is a skill that takes time to develop, but it is possible if we put all our care and vigilance from the beginning. Little by little, we will become more intuitive and sensitive to the energies present around us.

It is important to realize that our objective should not be to get rid of the lost soul in order to free the victim. It is also about helping a spiritual brother who is lost or confused. Therefore, we must treat them with love and patience, not paying attention to the gestures or voice changes they may have.

Below, I will share some recommendations that can help us find—if there is one—a parasitic spirit attached to our client. Later on, in chapter XXI, we will see how to work with them in order to help them leave in the light.

Spiritual Scanning

Let us suppose that, during the course of the session, we have not come across any lost soul. Then, it would be advisable, before bringing the person out of the hypnotic trance, to ask them to do a spiritual scan. This is a sweep, a kind of visualization of his or her vibratory field to detect if there is anything that might be out of place.

This is one of the easiest and most effective ways to do it. I have used it on countless occasions with excellent results. Let's remember that a person in a trance state can see, feel, and perceive things that he or she would not normally be able to in a normal state of consciousness.

Steps of spiritual scanning:

1. Ask to visualize the energetic or spiritual body.
2. Ask if they see any shadows, spots, or anything that is out of place, or if they feel anything different on any part of the body.
3. Once the area is identified, ask them to describe how it looks or feels.
4. Let them know that we will bring to their mind what they have found so that they can express themself.

5. Touch the part of the body where the shadow or sensation is located and drag the hand along the body until it reaches the head.
6. Touching their forehead, say: "brother, you can express yourself now".

Other Ways in Which They Manifest

When facilitating a session, we have to be alert, paying attention to any event that makes us suspect that something is not right or does not make sense as we work with our client.

- **Sudden Pain in Any Part of the Body**

  In this case, the key word is 'sudden'. This is a sensation that was not present at the beginning of the session and was not mentioned during the interview. Many times, the discomfort will be related to the part of the body where the spirit or spirits are attached, or to their death, that is, to the agony of their body.

  If we recall María's session, in "César's Message", which I narrated at the beginning of the explanation of the spiritual assistance technique, we will find that the spirits of César and Raúl manifested themselves through an intense foot pain that was related to the way in which César's body had died.

- **Headache and Pressure in Parts of the Body**

  On multiple occasions it has happened that, during the initial minutes of the hypnotic induction, my client begins to feel intense pain or pressure in the head. They have also felt pressure in the chest, belly, or heart.

  Why do they experience this symptom that was not present before, just at this moment? It may be that the attached spirit wants to prevent the session from developing, to prevent the person from entering into an expanded state of consciousness, where it will be practically impossible for him or her to continue hiding.

  It may be, on the contrary, that the level of trance that the person is achieving in the session, begins to prevent the spirit from going unnoticed, causing it to manifest.

  I remember one session with a young woman who began to feel a severe headache as soon as we started the induction. I knew there was something else going on and decided not to pay attention to it until the process was complete so we could begin to visit sad memories.

The young woman could not concentrate. She was telling me that her mind was blank, that no memory was coming to her mind and that her head was hurting so much. At that point, I asked her to lend her mind and lips to that headache so it could express itself. After asking them a couple of questions, a spirit communicated while crying and told me that they had died very young when they still had a lot of things to do in life.

- **The Person Sees a Light or Shadow**

  It is not uncommon to hear a person in trance say that they see a shadow that has approached them or that they feel that a light is blocking them. Some lost souls choose to present themselves in this way, as if getting in the way of what the person has to see or experience in the session.

- **A Supposed Past Life**

  As I mentioned earlier, there will be times when the spirit will not let us know that it is the spirit that is taking control of the conversation, making it difficult to know that we are no longer talking to the client in trance.

  Since there are spirits that have not realized that their body has died, when we are giving instructions or asking questions to our clients, the one who is actually answering will be the lost soul.

  This also applies in navigating past lives. There will be times when the client goes to a supposed past life of theirs, but, to our surprise, when the spirit has left that body that died and we ask them if they are going to the light, the answer will be, "I don't see the light". If we ask them where they decide to go now that they are spirit and they answer floating around, to the countryside, or staying at home, it may be a clear indication that the past life we thought was our client's is actually that of a lost soul attached to them that decided to take control of the communication.

  Logically, in order to reincarnate, we must first go to the light, meet with our guide, evaluate the reincarnation that recently ended, and join our spiritual group to begin planning the next reincarnation.

Upon discovering that it is a parasitic spirit, we can then ask for clarification of what is happening by asking if the one we are talking to is our client in a past life or someone who is with them.

- **Answers Out of Context**

  Another sign that alerts us that we may be communicating with a spirit or that it is intervening in our dialogue with the person in trance, are the answers out of context.

  There will be times when the answers will have nothing to do with the question asked to the person in trance. This was clearly seen during María's session, where both César and Raúl's soul began to answer my questions in an interspersed manner, rendering them meaningless.

  For example, when I asked César if he knew María's aunt, he said no, but, when I asked him why he wanted to meet her, his response was "I feel like she was my wife."

  This did not make any sense. What happened here is that while asking questions to César, who had been the husband of María's aunt in a past life and was there to give her a message, Raúl intervened, also causing confusion. This passage can be found in "César's Message." Something we must keep in mind is that there will be times when we will find more than one lost soul attached to our client and they will not take turns to dialogue with us. Only by being attentive to the answers they give us, will we be able to detect and understand them.

- **Dates Out of Range**

  Just as we should pay attention to answers or words that do not make sense, it is also important to pay attention to dates mentioned in the interview, such as dates of birth, and others that are mentioned during the session.

  If I ask a client in trance who is 30 years old to go to a sad memory, and when I ask them how old they are in that memory and they tell me they are 50 years old, there are two options: my client is in a past life or I am talking to a lost soul attached to them.

After this, we must ask more questions to clear doubts or continue navigating that past life and see if, after the body dies, the spirit goes to the light or not.

- **Obstacles**

  On several occasions, the lost souls I have communicated with during a hypnosis session let me know that they had been waiting for me. Some even told me that they knew who I was and that they were waiting for me to help them go to the light.

  Others knew the session was going to take place and were not very happy about it. What happened some of those times, before the session, was that my clients experienced all kinds of obstacles and setbacks to get to the appointment. These souls knew what was going to happen during the work with me and wanted to prevent it at all costs.

  In these cases, my recommendation is to ask those clients to come to the session no matter what. Do not let anyone or anything stop them. Remember to be careful not to share your suspicions with them because fear may prevent them from cooperating.

A Builder at the Tower of Babel

As I mentioned above, there are different ways in which a lost soul can manifest during a hypnosis session, and the person to whom it is attached does not necessarily have to be in a trance to be able to communicate with it. There are times when the energy of this lost soul is so pervasive in the vibratory field of the victim that they can manifest at will and without the need for the victim to be in an altered state of consciousness.

This was the case with Shania, who was referred to me by one of the people who had taken my Introspective Hypnosis course. Shania had come to her for help because she felt that a supposed demonic entity had possessed her. She told her that this entity's harassment had started years ago and that the situation was getting worse, to the point of not letting her live in peace.

While they were in the initial interview, Shania began screaming at the top of her lungs and out of control, so much so that her sister had to intervene to calm her down. It was at this point that the practitioner who was going to facilitate the session decided that this was a complicated case for her to handle and told Shania's sister that I was equipped to guide the session. Hours later, Shania scheduled a session with me.

During our initial interview, she gave me the details of when she had begun to perceive the symptoms of possession. She told me that she had been having recurring nightmares and had felt an energy taking control of her at any moment. Shania was so afraid of what might happen in the session that she would not let go of control during the induction.

Knowing that trance is not necessary in these cases, I asked Shania to allow the spirit to manifest through her. She flatly refused because of the fear she felt. After a few minutes of trying to convince her and making her understand that, if we did not work with this spirit, she would continue to experience these problems, she agreed and began to let go of control little by little.

When I told the spirit that it could express itself, Shania started making strange noises and shouting in some kind of language that I did not understand. As I thanked the spirit for initiating communication and tried to ask them a few questions, they began to vocalize some sort of chanting without paying attention to my questions, as if trying to intimidate me.

I tried for a couple of minutes to get them to answer me, but the spirit just kept on with the same attitude, imitating a supposed demon. At this point, I told them that if they shouted I could not understand them, so I decided to remain silent until they calmed down, but, as soon as I asked a question, they started again with the screaming and chanting.

This time, I became more firm and told them that if they continued shouting I would not speak to them, and that if they did not communicate in English, I would not speak to them either. They tried again and again to intimidate me with their shouting, but my reaction was only to tell them very calmly that I did not understand them and that I was not going to talk to them if they continued like that.

Seeing that their behavior had no effect on me and did not frighten me, they began to cry and I was able to start a dialogue with them.

Antonio: I'm here to help you. Do you want me to help you or not?

Lost Soul: Yes, I want you to help me.

A: "Okay, so, to begin with, I need you to stop shouting because I don't understand anything you are saying to me. I also need you to speak to me in English so I can understand what you are saying. Are you a man or a woman?" I asked, referring to when they had a body.

LS: "I am a man!" he said, opening his eyes as he looked at me and lifted his torso off the bed.

A: What happened to your body, brother, how did it die?

LS: "I died, but I don't know how," he answered, gesturing with his hands and opening his eyes.

A: Do you remember what happened to your body? This is important to know.

At this point, he began again to rant in another language.

A: If you don't speak English, I can't understand what you are saying. If you keep talking like that, you are wasting your time. Communicate in English and I'll help you, okay? You are stuck there, yes or no?

LS: "Yes," he replied, clenching his fist and leaning his torso forward, as he wept and wailed, "I'm trapped!"

A: I'm here to help you, but I need you to calm down. How did your body die? Do you remember?

LS: My body never died. It is in hell.

A: Shania is a woman and you are a man. How come you are in a woman's body if your body never died? Also, you say your body is in hell. I don't believe there is a hell. Tell me why you are with Shania.

LS: I was sent to kill her.

A: Are you saying you were sent to kill her?

LS: You don't believe in hell?

A: No, not at all. That's in your mind, you say they sent you?

LS: Yes, to kill her.

A: I am trying to understand. You are spirit and you are free, so how can someone send you to do things?

Again, the spirit began his chanting, trying to show that he was not interested in what I was asking.

A: If you continue to make those noises, I'm not going to talk to you. Let me know when you're ready for further conversation. You said you were sent, right?

LS: "Yes," he answered in tears, "yes!"

A: This is what I want to understand. Someone used you and sent you to Shania and now you're trapped. Do you think that person who sent you cares about you? Does it seem fair what they did?

The spirit started screaming again and not paying attention to me.

A: If you keep yelling, I'm not going to talk to you. You let me know when you're done. You could spend years and years stuck in there. That will be your problem.

LS: We were building Babylon.

A: And what happened to you while you were building Babylon?

LS: I fell.

A: And, when you fell, which part of your body hit the ground first? Which part suffered the most?

LS: "I can't breathe!" he uttered in agitation.

I tried to figure out which part of the body was suffering the most, trying to determine what symptom it might be causing Shania, but the spirit just cried and wailed in another language.

LS: That's why she likes languages!

A: Does she like languages because of you?

LS: "I'm going to leave my family! I fell off the tower!" he exclaimed ig- noring my previous question.

This is what was holding the spirit on this plane: his family and not wanting to get away from them. He had not realized that this had hap- pened a long time ago.

A: Calm down and pay attention to what I say. You are not going to leave your family. What died was your body, but you are spirit and spirit never dies. This means that you are not going to leave your family because you can still be with them in spirit. This happened in Babylon, a long time ago, if you think about our time. Your family may be in the light and looking for you and waiting for you. You are just wasting your time as you continue to be glued to Shania.

Communication with this spirit lasted a few more minutes. We were able to find out what his body felt when he died and which of these symptoms were present in Shania. In the end, he decided to go to the light and leave Shania's body, but not before working on forgiveness for the symptoms he had caused her for years.

When the spirit withdrew, Shania came back to herself. The expression on her face had changed drastically, showing great tranquility.

Testing the Spirits

As we have seen previously, during the hypnotic trance state, lost souls can manifest in different ways. Each one of them has a reason or motivation for having attached itself to the person who came to the session or for approaching and expressing itself upon seeing that there is an individual in an altered state of consciousness.

Some will say they are there to help, a few to guide, and several others will claim to be the person's mother, father, sister, or brother, when in fact they are not. There will also be lost souls who will pretend to be spirit guides or the client's light beings, and even dare to give messages and make predictions.

The ones we should be more careful with are those that appeal to our ego so that we leave them alone. Let us remember that a spirit can have a lot of information about us from the dimension in which it is. It can tell us the color of our aura, our level of evolution based on that color and whether or not we are afraid during the communication.

Thanks to that information, spirits can make us feel special with phrases like "the color of your energy is advanced, "you are a guide," or "I see that in a past life you were so and so." This is not to say that this is not true, but we should be cautious in how we react to such words. If we take the bait and play along, we will end up focusing on a series of questions around us, completely missing the therapeutic purpose of our work with our clients. We must never forget that they (the client) have the lead role, not us.

Unfortunately, I have witnessed how hypnotists and therapists use their clients or patients, like encyclopedias, to obtain data that was only useful for them, keeping the person in trance for a prolonged period of time without need.

If we understand our work from the view of spirituality, we will know that we have in front of us a reincarnated spirit (our client) in search of help, guidance, and relief. Therefore, we should never approach a session of this type from our ego or for our own interest. This is the first thing I teach in my courses.

So, based on what was explained above, it is essential to feel out the spirits that claim to be there for some positive or favorable purpose for our client. But, how to check what a spirit says that we cannot see?

I think this Bible passage may give us some clues:

Matthew 7:15-20

15 Watch out for false prophets. They come to you in sheep's clothing, but inwardly they are ferocious wolves.

16 By their fruit you will recognize them. Do people pick grapes from thornbushes, or figs from thistles?

17 Likewise, every good tree bears good fruit, but a bad tree bears bad fruit.

18 A good tree cannot bear bad fruit, and a bad tree cannot bear good fruit.

19 Every tree that does not bear good fruit is cut down and thrown into the fire.

20 Thus, by their fruit you will recognize them.

Well, this is exactly how we will be able to do it, recognizing them through their fruits.

Spirits Posing as Guides

While this case is not too common, it has happened to me enough times to include it in the list.

We must keep in mind that communication with a spiritual guide is one of love, hope and compassion. Their messages are always aimed at understanding, clarifying doubts about certain lessons we are facing and, above all, seeking our spiritual evolution.

The dialogue with a guide is beautiful, without predictions or negative judgments towards the other. They will never say that they must be attached to us to make sure we do things right, nor will they tell us what we have to do—as this would interfere with our free will—nor will they interfere in our spiritual evolution, or in the therapeutic work we do with clients.

There have been times when, during communication with a true being of light, the tone and cadence of the voice was completely transformed, as was the expression on the face of the person through whom it manifested. When a true being of light communicates with us, you can feel the change of energy in the environment and the vibration of love in their words.

To be sure that we are talking to a spiritual guide, it is advisable to ask them a few questions and feel the answers they give us:

Can you give me the definition of love?

Who is God?

Who is Jesus?

What is spiritual evolution?

What is the purpose of reincarnation?

What are spirits?

In the end, these are just a few examples that will allow us to determine if the answers come from love, compassion, and evolution. These, basically, will help us reveal whether or not we are dealing with an evolved spirit.

Spirits Impersonating Loved Ones

Some lost spirits, whether or not attached to the person being treated, may show up at the session pretending to be a deceased loved one.

Whether it is the mother, father, sister, or grandfather, we must remember that spirits have access to a lot of information while they are in that dimension so it should not surprise us that, if they show up in the same physical form, they may even present the wound they suffered in their physical body before they left. I myself have been amazed at this type of case.

What I advise to do in this situation is for the client to feel—not just see—the energy of that spirit manifesting. We humans can recognize our loved ones by their energy or frequency. I usually ask my clients to determine if they feel that spirit as someone familiar or not.

The spirit of a true loved one will manifest with the same type of personality they had when they inhabited the Earth, indeed, they may give specific details of events that only they and the other person knew about.

Spirits Claiming to Come to Help

It may be true that, during the trance, some spirits come to help their loved ones or have been attached to them with that intention. As we will see later, people who have been abused since childhood are the most likely to have spirits attached to their aura. They unknowingly send a distress signal to the universe by attracting spirits who have the intention to help, as in Cristina's session in "A Spirit in the House."

When these types of scenarios arise, what I do is ask my client if they remember at any time asking for help. If their answer is no, then I tell the spirit that their help is no longer needed and work with them so that they can go to the light.

Spirits Claiming to Be Satan or Demons

One of the methods that certain souls will use with us is to generate fear, assuring us that they are demons, Satan, Lucifer, or 'the evil one'.

This is often accompanied by gestures, voice changes, and violent movements. Their intention is to scare us into leaving them alone and stop interrogating them. Many lost souls are afraid to deal with their unfinished business. As they still maintain their ego, personality, and beliefs, it is very common for them to be terrified of being judged or sent to hell for what they have done, depending on their beliefs.

It is important not to be afraid in these cases, nor to react negatively to what they say. In my case, some have told me, "I know what you want to do and you are not going to get me out of here." My response is always that this is not my objective and that they can stay as long as necessary. I reply that I just want to talk to them to understand what happened to them and why they decided to stay here. Others have told me, "She's mine and I'm not letting her go," to which I reply that if she is yours, why haven't you taken her already? Some have responded that it is not time yet.

My intention with these replies is not to disrespect them, but to make them understand that what they are saying makes no sense and that, in reality, they are the ones who are trapped there and not my client.

Spirits Using Well-Known and Rrevered Names

There will be times when spirits will present themselves using names of well-known personages, such as Julius Caesar, Napoleon, or even archangels, Jesus, or the Virgin Mary.

We must be careful with them because what they seek is to impress us so that we ask them other types of questions, diverting us from the work we should be doing with them. Later on, we will see how we can test the spirits to know how to proceed with them.

***

When communicating with lost souls, we must be intelligent and careful about the details that are presented. We must let them know that they are welcome, that we are not there to judge or expel them and we just want to talk to them to understand what happened to them.

Not feeling threatened by our presence, they will be able to lower their guard and engage in a dialogue with us.

The Supplanting Spirit

Steve's father had died in a car accident when he was a child. While in a trance, in one of the first memories he came back to, he saw a coffin where his father was supposed to be, but when he tried to get closer to see it in detail, he could not see his father's face. This seemed strange to me.

Steve assumed that his dad did not want him to see him because of the way his face had looked after the accident. Actually, this explanation did not make much sense to me. This spirit would present itself again near the end of the session.

That day we also found a lost soul attached to his partner. She had died in a car accident and could not see the light when she left the body. When I asked her at what point she had attached herself to the body of Steve's wife, Lydia, she replied that she didn't remember, that she only saw a cemetery with many gravestones.

I asked her if she knew whose tombstone it was and she said no, that she couldn't see it because it was very old, but she could see her picture there. She even said that it was obvious that the photo had been cropped and that it looked like she was with someone else who did not love her. She was bringing to understand that they had done a work of witchcraft on her.

After this, we helped her to go to the light, but, before leaving, she informed us that there was something dark about Steve and his wife. It was then that we decided to ask the spirit of Steve's grandfather, named Frank, for help.

Steve: I can see that.

Antonio: I'm going to count from three to one and you change. Three, two, one. Good afternoon, Mr. Frank. Can you help us with something I am going to ask you?

Frank: Yes.

A: What is stopping Lydia from being happy? There seems to be something blocking her. The spirit that was attached to her told me there was a black shadow. Can you tell me what is going on?

F: Something black.

A: And, where is that black thing located?

F: There, near them.

A: Can you ask that black thing to identify themself?

F: "No," he replied, shaking his head.

A: Who can help us with that? Can your son help us?

F: "Something bad," he said without answering my question. "It's very heavy. His (Steve's) dad is here."

After talking a bit with Grandpa and asking him a few questions, we said our goodbyes. We were ready to engage in communication with Steve's father.

A: One, two, three. Good afternoon, Richard.

Steve: He does not want to connect.

A: Ask your father if there is anything we can help him with.

S: "He won't talk to me," he replied with tears in his eyes.

A: Then, take a good look. What you are telling me doesn't make sense.

S: "He doesn't want to," he said, interrupting me.

A: Wait. It may not be your father. I want you at this moment to ask the one who appears to be your father to turn around and look you in the eye. Ask him with authority.

Steve started crying and breathing rapidly. Apparently, he had seen something that had frightened him.

A: Relax and cover yourself with light. What are you seeing?

S: "Ugly!" he uttered.

A: Ask them who they are.

S: They won't turn around.

A: Ask them if they are the dark thing over Lydia.

S: They're ugly!

A: Sure, because they're not your dad. That's why they didn't want to look at you. Ask them to identify themself.

S: No, they're gone. I am very afraid.

The spirit pretending to be Steve's father left and did not appear again during the session. How did they know that Steve's father had been disfigured in the accident? How was it possible that they could take Steve's father's form to the point of confusion? How did they know that if they looked into Steve's eyes, Steve would realize that they were not his father?

It is difficult to know the answers to these questions, but, as I always tell my clients while they are navigating a past life, the eyes are the windows to the soul. You only have to look at that person to know if they are or will be in your current life. Apparently, looking into someone's eyes makes them identifiable no matter if they are in another body.

I wonder if they are seeing the eyes, the soul, or the energy.

A Dore Loser

Vicky came to the session looking to remove blocks she was experiencing in her life. She wanted to know if, on a subconscious level, there was something that was keeping her from moving forward or causing her to sabotage herself.

Every business she undertook started well, but quickly deteriorated. The same happened with her love life. She could not maintain a relationship for long because her partners would end the relationship without any explanation.

Working on her session, Vicky began to experience a pain in her heart that had not been present before the session, nor was it mentioned during the interview. The situation made me suspect that there was an energy; a lost soul that wanted to manifest. Dragging the pain from her heart into her mind with my hand, I indicated that they could now express themself.

Vicky: Oh, my heart, my God, it hurts!

Antonio: Have you been with Vicky for a long or short time?

Lost Soul: Oh, it's all green, I see space!

A: How long have you been with her?

LS: "Her whole life," they replied, shaking their head from side to side.

A: Who are you?

LS: I am her other half.

A: So, if you are her other half and you are together, why is she feeling that pain?

LS: "Give me a minute. This is beautiful, there are crystals," they said moving their head in every direction, as if they were seeing something.

A: Where do you see those crystals?

LS: Inside her.

Again, their answers made no sense.

A: My question is what are you doing with her. She is feeling tense and sore, what are you doing with her?

LS: She is tough. She's healing.

A: Healing from what or whom.

LS: Us.

A: Who do you mean by us?

LS: We are one: male and female. She keeps us together.

His explanations still made no sense to me.

A: So she keeps you together and that's how you two are healing. Is that correct?

LS: "Yes," he nodded, "and, we are healing her as well."

A: So, let me ask you a question. If you are healing her, why does she feel that pain?

LS: Because it is a complicated process.

At this point, I knew I was communicating with a lost soul who was trying to confuse me with his answers to keep me from realizing who he really was. I decided to play along to see where he wanted to take me.

A: So what is the plan?

LS: Healing.

A: Three, two, one. Vicky, have you noticed that there is an energy there that says it is healing you? Do you think that is the case?

V: "There's something there," she replied in a soft voice, shaking her head from side to side.

A: Are you feeling well?

V: It feels comfortable, but weird.

A: We all have free will. Do you want to tell this energy to go away or stay there?

V: I am curious. The pain is gone.

A: So you want to keep it there?

V: Yes, because he is trying to heal me.

A: "All right, brother," I said, referring to the lost soul, "Vicky has given you permission to stay."

At that point, I knew I would keep asking him questions to expose him.

LS: Of course!

A: But, you have to take away that discomfort she feels.

LS: She just has to relax. She's tense.

A: Can you give her any advice or message?

LS: That she has to feel me.

A: Can you help her with her self-esteem?

LS: Yes.

A: Can you help her heal her back?

LS: I am healing it.

This energy wanted me to believe that he was helping her with everything; that he could cure her of her ills and that it was just a matter of her relaxing. From his voice and gestures, I could tell that my questions were making him desperate. That was my goal.

A: How can she know that you are healing her? Can you give her a sign?

LS: Yes, it's a process through the whole body. . She is going to feel a little discomfort, but that's okay.

A: How can she realize that you are healing her?

LS: The process is different every time.

A: Let me ask you a question: do you know anything about her past lives?

With that question, the lost soul was silent for a few seconds as if in thought and stopped shaking his head.

A: Or should I ask her to go to a past life to look for information?

With this question, he became more desperate and his breathing became more agitated.

LS: I'm trying to get her to relax more. She's getting tense and she's trying to keep me out. She's tough.

A: I need to talk to her again to continue working. If I work with her, you benefit too, right?

LS: "She laughs because she's not in control," he said, smiling, sighing, and shaking his head, "I'm in control."

That was the key. That energy had begun to show itself as it was.

A: Oh no, no, no, no. I didn't like what you just said. How can you be in control if this is her body? Do you realize that? You are just a guest in that body. What you just said worries me. How can you be in control of someone you want to help?

LS: It's part of the process.

A: Can you tell me who Jesus was?

LS: Not that. No.

A: Can you give me the definition of God; does it sound familiar?

LS: No.

A: Now I understand who you really are, do you realize that? I'm going to ask you to leave her alone. You are causing her pain and discomfort. You are there for no reason, you should continue your path of evolution. If you realize, you're not doing anything with her, you're just wasting your time. You are just wasting your time. How long have you been there and trying to do what? Would you consider going to the light today?

LS: "No," he replied in annoyance.

So, I continued the conversation with this energy for a few more minutes. As I asked him and Vicky questions, I was able to find out that they had been a couple in a past life, in which she left him for another man. So, by way of revenge, he decided to attach to her and cause her trouble. It was this energy that made all her business dealings go wrong and drove away any suitor who approached her.

I spent a long time trying to get her to forgive what happened in that other life. The spirit resisted going into the light, to the point of shaking Vicky's body violently, like a scene from a horror movie, because he wanted me to leave him alone.

After talking for several more minutes, the two agreed to solve their problem in the light and the spirit agreed to detach from Vicky.

SYMPTOMS CAUSED BY PARASITIC SPIRITS

As offensive as the term 'parasite' may seem, in part, it defines very well their way of acting. These lost souls not only cause ills in the affected person, but also live off their energy, causing them chronic exhaustion.

It is difficult to establish a standard or list of ailments that a lost soul can cause in its victim. To give us an idea, let us think of all the physical, psychological, and emotional manifestations that we ourselves may have in our present body. In the same way that each of us has a story behind each symptom, lost souls have their own stories behind each symptom, with the difference that they will also have, in addition, ailments related to the agony of their body before they die.

For example, if the body of the lost soul died on the gallows, it will not only have the pain that the noose inflicted on the neck, but may also experience shortness of breath, fear, anger at being hanged in front of an audience, and the worry that it leaves a family behind.

By this I mean that if one of these lost souls were to attach itself to the aura or vibratory field of a person, it is very possible that the person would experience in his or her body the same symptoms that the soul had when it still had a body.

Does that mean, then, that the person affected by that lost soul will feel those ailments from the moment of attachment? Not necessarily. Let us remember that a trauma awakens when we face a situation similar to the event that originated it. This trauma, which was stored in our subconscious, will make us react in the same way we did the first time, no matter how much time has passed.

It may also happen that, at the time the person was affected by the spiritual attachment, they were facing a situation similar to the one faced by the lost soul when they had a body. By identifying this event as their own, the lost soul will trigger all the symptoms they suffered at that time. Both spirits will experience whatever harms and impacts the other.

Let's go one step further. Understanding the origin of our symptoms can be even more complex if we think about soul entrapment, where part of our energy is trapped in previously lived experiences, which were not properly processed at the physical, emotional, and mental levels.

That part of our energy trapped, usually in events related to the agony of the body, is reliving that event over and over again, making us feel in our present body what we felt in that past body.

Then, the symptoms caused by the lost souls, together with those caused by our own soul entrapment, and, adding those that do have a medical explanation and are not related to the two previous scenarios is what generates a greater complexity in the regressive hypnosis session. Even more so, if we take into account that a person can have more than one lost soul attached to them at the same time, as in the case of María—in "César's Message"—who had three energies attached to her causing all kinds of discomfort.

(Symptom of the lost soul × number of souls attached) + symptom of our own entrapment + physical symptoms = total symptoms in the affected person.

Taking into account all of the above, it is easy to understand why medicine cannot find a logical explanation for all the symptoms that human beings present, whether it is a constant rash, claustrophobia or a strong stage fright. These manifestations may have come from a past life, but they may also come from a spirit attached to us.

The complexity of this scenario is that a physician, not knowing these concepts, will label their patient based on the ailments they are experiencing, without even being able to explain the true origin of the ailments.

For example, I remember the case of a young woman I treated a few years ago. She suffered from a severe skin allergy on her hands, which flared up whenever she was under a lot of stress. Despite having visited several doctors of different specialties, she had not been able to get relief through the treatments they had established for her.

Being in a trance, I asked her to go to the moment when this skin problem originated. Immediately, she began to tell me that she was in the main square of a small town, in front of a bonfire. All around, there were many spectators. Her father, who was one of the authorities of that town, wanted to set an example to everyone by burning his own daughter's hands for stealing.

So, in this life, every time she felt emotionally the same way she felt in that reincarnation, her soul remembered it and made her hands react as if they were being burned again. Her soul had been trapped in that experience and she relived it over and over again.

On the other hand, if we think about another possible scenario, an individual could be clinically diagnosed as bipolar or schizophrenic when, in reality, they could be experiencing the influence of a lost soul attached to their aura. This soul could cause them to change moods, hear voices, or behave as if there were two totally different people in one body.

And, if we look at this scenario from a religious point of view, not knowing what a lost soul is, it is very possible that the diagnosis is that of demonic possession and the affected person is sent for an exorcism.

I will now mention some of the symptoms that my clients have suffered from having one or more lost souls attached to them:

- Grief related to the manner of death
- Suicidal thoughts
- Changes in temperament

- Recurrent nightmares
- Feeling that they are not themselves at times
- Depression
- Residual emotions
- Being avoided by others
- Listening to voices
- Fears
- Phobias
- Skin reactions
- Fatigue
- Feeling of being observed

The Suicidal Spirit

When I met Mónica, she was twenty-three years old and had been diagnosed with schizophrenia. She began hearing voices when she was a child, while looking in the mirror. This voice, which came from a lost soul, told her that she was good for nothing and that her parents didn't love her.

Even though this soul was not attached to her energetic body, it somehow made her experience what they had felt when they had a body and influenced the way she thought and behaved.

While in a hypnotic trance, she returned to one of those memories in which the mirror spoke to her.

Mónica: I am in my room.

Antonio: Very good. So, what is happening?

M: I'm looking in the mirror and I start to hear a voice.

A: What does that voice tell you?

M: You think they love you, but they only pretend to. You're not going to be anybody in life.

A: And whose voice do you think it is?

M: I don't know. It's a young man's voice.

A: What clse is he telling you?

M: You're going to be a failure. No one is going to like you and you're good for nothing.

A: Do you believe any of the stupid things that voice has told you? Let's take an example, if I tell you that you are Chinese, does that make you Chinese?

M: No.

A: If I tell you that you are colored, does that make you colored?

M: No.

A: Then, why do you believe all the stupid things that voice is telling you? Do you believe that this is the voice of a spirit?

M: "Yes," she said to me with tears in her eyes.

A: I want you, spiritually, to visualize your body and tell me if everything is white or if you find any shadows attached to you.

M: Everything is white.

This indicated that, at least at that moment, the spirit was not attached to her.

A: If it is a spirit, it should be in the light, right?

M: Right.

A: We die, we go to the light, we evolve and then we come back with another body to continue on the path of evolution. It's about learning lessons, isn't it?

M: Right.

A: Let's think for a moment. Suppose you die of old age and, being able to go to the light to be with God, you waste your time going to a young woman's room to hide behind a mirror to tell her stupid things. Here you have a spirit telling you that you are a failure, when in fact he knows nothing. Who is the failure, then?

M: It's him!

A: And he's hiding there because he's afraid to follow his course. Does that make sense?

M: Yes.

A: Are we going to believe one of these spirits?

M: No.

A: What would you say to that spirit?

M: To stop.

A: If you are so powerful and so wise, evolve and go to the light. Are you going to tell me that I am a failure when you are the failure? Now, I'm going to count to three and you're going to ask that spirit if he's still here. One, two, three. Ask it.

M: He is not here.

A: So, that means he's not so powerful because he can't even leave your room. Look in the mirror and ask the spirit who he is and what his name is.

M: He says he won't tell me.

A: Ask him how he died.

M: He says he committed suicide.

Mónica also had suicidal thoughts. Now, we knew that they actually came from the young man's lost soul.

A: Do you realize who you are believing? He committed suicide, he failed, and now he wants you to do the same? Ask him why he committed suicide.

M: "He was alone," she said crying, as if she could feel his sorrow.

A: Ask him if I can talk to him. We are here to help you and him.

M: He tells me he doesn't want to.

A: "Do you realize that all those feelings and words belong to him? Because he is close to you, he makes you feel the same way, but it doesn't mean they are yours. Now, I'm going to count from three to one and talk to him. Three, two, one. You can express yourself now," I indicated, touching his forehead, "Have you been with Mónica for a long time or a short time?"

Lost Soul: For a long time.

A: Can you tell me your name?

LS: No.

A: Do you want me to name you for the time being?

LS: No.

A: I have to call you something. What can I call you?

LS: No one.

A: I can't call you that. For now, I'll call you brother, shall I?

LS: Okay.

A: All right, brother, tell me your story, what happened to you?

LS: I was a failure in life.

A: Why do you say that? What happened to you?

LS: They made fun of me.

A: Who were making fun of you?

LS: Everyone.

A: Why were they making fun of you?

LS: Because I wasn't good at anything.

A: For example?

LS: Getting along with other people.

A: Do you consider that you were a bad person? Did you have bad intentions towards people?

LS: Yes, I hated them.

A: But one doesn't hate for nothing. One hates when they do something to us, right?

LS: They made fun of me.

Up to this point, we already knew that he was the lost soul of a suicidal young man who was transmitting ideas and emotions to Mónica. As I continued to dig into his life story, I was able to find out that he felt like a failure not only because his friends made fun of him, but also because his parents treated him badly.

A: Forget what they told you. What I want to know is if you considered yourself a bad person.

LS: No

A: So, if you consider that you were not a bad person, why should you care what others thought of you. You have been influenced by those people who knew nothing about you and were cruel to you, right?

LS: Yes.

A: You are better than that. I understand that you were under pressure and decided to end your life. I'm not saying you took the easy way out because I know it was difficult and you still feel affected by it. Do you think that by killing yourself you solved anything?

LS: I didn't have to suffer anymore.

A: But, look where you are now. You're standing behind a mirror, talking to a young woman and asking her to do the same thing. You are generating karma by giving bad advice to a well-feeling young woman. Why would you want someone else to go through what you went through?

LS: So they know how I felt.

A: You don't have to make them feel that way for them to understand. I've never experienced anything like that myself, but I understand how you feel. That's why I'm here, to help you. Do you believe me?

M: No.

A: You can feel my energy. You know I am here to help you both.

M: I don't believe you.

A: So, if you don't believe me, I'm going to ask you to trust me. How can I help you to continue on your path? You need to evolve and go into the light and then come back with another body to continue learning your lessons. Does that make sense?

LS: Yes.

A: Very good. You want to show those who made fun of you that you're smart, right?

LS: Right.

A: Well, what do intelligent spirits do? Go into the light! I know you don't want Mónica to go through what you went through and do what you did, do you?

LS: No.

A: So you want her to go through this?

LS: Yes.

A: What's in it for you?

LS: That they understand how I have suffered.

A: Don't you think she's had a taste of that?

LS: No.

A: You have driven her to want to end her life.

LS: I almost made it.

A: Actually, you almost accumulated a huge debt for influencing people that way.

The spirit did not want to collaborate with me, but I still had to find out why it had chosen Mónica among so many other souls. So I asked her to find out if they had met in a past life, and they did.

In a life that had taken place 85 years ago, the same one in which he committed suicide, they had been good friends. She had been the only one who paid attention to him. For that reason, he had searched for her through time, even though she was now in another body.

After discovering this, I asked the spirit how it was possible for him to treat the only person who had ever cared about him this way. He replied that he wanted her to commit suicide as well so they could be together. After Mónica and I had a dialogue with him, the spirit realized his mistake. He apologized to her for the trouble he had caused her and decided to continue on his way in the light.

Every lost soul has a reason to produce symptoms and influence the life of another soul.

The Soldier Who Was Not Aware of His Death

Jossie came to my door looking to have an Introspective Hypnosis session at her husband's insistence. He had been following my YouTube channel for some time and was confident that this type of tool could help his wife.

During our initial interview, Jossie told me all about her childhood and what she had experienced through her mother. These emotions had accumulated along with other recent ones related to her marriage, causing her great anguish and deep sorrow. "I need to get it all out," she told me through tears as we talked.

Other symptoms she mentioned were dizziness and nausea, which she had been experiencing for several years. The doctors had not found a logical explanation for these discomforts and the tests she had undergone had not yielded any positive results. The dizziness she suffered was so severe that it made her lose her balance, depriving her of a normal life.

In trance, Jossie visited different events from her childhood. As she reviewed them, we worked on forgiving her mother, helping her to change her perception of what had happened, and to understand the reason for the experience. The altered state of consciousness she was in was so deep that her eyelids kept moving, so much so that it seemed as if her eyes were open.

We were able to communicate with the Higher Self of her mother, who was still alive. She was able to give us her side of the story, as well as why she was acting this way. The mother apologized to her.

After removing the negative emotion associated with the events she experienced, we were able to begin working on the symptom of dizziness. I asked her to go back to the last time she had experienced that symptom.

Antonio: Jossie, I want you to go to a memory where you felt dizzy. Five, four, three, two, one. You're already there.

What I was intending with this was to help her to make conscious what, for her at that moment, was unconscious. The symptom will always be the thread that will lead us to the origin of the symptom.

Jossie: I'm walking down the stairs, feel the dizziness and grab the handrail.

A: That's right. Now, I want you to feel that dizziness more intensely. One, more intense. Two, even more intense. Three, more intense. That dizziness feels like what?

J: Like a headache.

A: That's right! And, that headache feels similar to what, as if it were happening to your head?

J: It gives me pressure.

A: Now, I'm going to count from three to one and I want you to go back to the moment when you are feeling that pressure in your head. Three, two, one. Like you know, even if you think you're imagining it, where do you think you are as you feel pressure on your head?

J: I cannot see.

This answer made me suspect that this condition did not come from her.

A: Then, feel and go backwards and backwards, back to the first time you felt the dizziness. One, two, three. You're already there.

J: I was lying down and I had a dream. It was like something wanted to possess me.

A: What does that 'something' look like?

J: It just doesn't have a shape, it doesn't have anything. It's just like something that wants to pull me into it.

At this point, I was almost certain that this was not a dream, but an event she had experienced while her body was asleep, while she was in the astral plane.

A: I understand, so I'm going to count from three to one and I want you to lend them your mind and your lips to talk to them. Three, two, one. Brother, thank you for today's communication, have you been there for a long or short time?

Lost Soul: A long time!

Antonio: When you had a body, were you a man or a woman?

LS: "Man," he replied in a deeper voice.

A: Brother, what happened? How did your body die?

LS: I don't know.

A: No problem. Let me ask you a question, why are you with Jossie?

LS: She is very weak.

A: And, because she is very weak, are you going to go up to her and attach to her? Are there any symptoms that you have caused her voluntarily or involuntarily?

LS: Possibly.

A: We are going to remember how your body died. I'm going to count from three to one and you're going to go to the last moment you had a body. Three, two, one. You're already there. Tell me what comes to your mind. What's going on?

LS: I'm in a war, but I'm hiding. When I peek out, they shoot me in the head.

Therein laid the source of Jossie's symptom, what the spirit was making her feel.

A: And what do you feel when the bullet hits your head?

LS: Nothing, I just fall.

A: I ask you another question, did you realize that your body died?

LS: "No," he answered very confidently.

A: Have you realized that you are communicating through a body that is not yours?

LS: Yes.

A: That means you are not in your body. That body died. What is it that keeps you from going into the light today, brother?

LS: I don't know.

This type of amnesia is very common in lost souls.

A: I want you to go back to the moment of impact. Three, two, one. You take the bullet and your body falls. I want you to feel how your spirit leaves the body. You must understand that, with the death of that body, that experience is over forever. Pay attention and tell me what you see as you leave the body.

LS: My family.

A: What about your family?

LS: I don't want to leave them.

This was the reason why he had not been able to go to the light after he passed away.

A: Who are you leaving behind?

LS: My parents, my children, and wife.

A: And, then, because you don't want to leave them behind, what do you decide to do?

LS: I can't believe I'm not going to be with them anymore. I don't want to.

A: But, only the body has died. You are spirit and spirit does not die. Talk to them, explain to them what has happened to you. Tell them that now you have to leave, but that you will always be with them in spirit, that you are not abandoning them.

LS: "I don't want to," she sighed.

A: So, if you don't want to, what are you going to do, are you going to stay there? Because, if you stay there, what's in it for you? You've attached to Jossie and you're making her dizzy and nauseous. What have you accomplished with that? Are you even with your family?

LS: No.

A: You have accomplished nothing. Rather, you have unintentionally harmed her. Now, that your body has died in that war, I want you to travel in spirit to where they are. You are free and you can fly wherever you want. Go and talk to your children.

LS: But how, if they can't see me?

A: Oh, they are not going to see you. You feel love for them. Have you ever seen love?

LS: Yes.

A: What is love like, what color is it, what shape is it, what does it smell like? We don't see it, we feel it. You can communicate through the mind. They are spirit and so are you. What do you want to tell them?

LS: That I love them very much, that I think of them and that they will always have a very special place in my heart. And, even though I am no longer with them in body, I will always be by their side.

A: In spirit, that's it! And, tell them that you have to go, but that they will be fine because you are going to watch them from there. You are going to take care of them.

LS: I have to go. Don't cry for me anymore. Let me go.

Those last words were very revealing, since, many times, our sadness is what traps the souls of our loved ones and does not let them leave.

A: And why are you telling them to leave you? Is their crying keeping you here?

LS: They cry a lot for me.

A: What is your name, brother?

LS: José.

A: And, what war were you fighting in?

LS: I don't remember, but I was wearing a blue uniform.

A: What do your children say to you, now that you have just spoken to them?

LS: They just smile.

A: Very good. Now, before you go into the light, notice when it was that you attached to Jossie. What was going on in her life?

LS: She had a lot of problems, she fought a lot with her husband.

A: Very good. So, now ask her to forgive you for having attached yourself to her body. Look at all that you have caused her unnecessarily.

LS: I want to apologize for this damage I have caused you. It was not my intention. I did not want to accept that I was no longer in this world.

A: That's right. Jossie, do you want to forgive José?

J: "Yes," she replied, changing her voice.

A: José, there where you are, now that you have asked for forgiveness and your children are smiling, see if someone comes for you or if you see a light.

LS: Yes, I see it far away.

A: That's right. Go to it. Let's ask God, according to the religion you had, that, with his infinite mercy, he sends a ray of light for you to return home.

LS: "I'm getting closer," he said with a sigh and a calm face.

Thus José's spirit departed, but not before I asked him to take all his symptoms with him so that Jossie could regain full control of her body.

The session lasted a few more minutes. When Jossie came out of the trance, she had no memory of what had happened, nor of the communication with José's spirit. She told me that she felt very relaxed, and her face reflected it. Now, she looked radiant and smiling.

WHO ARE MORE SUSCEPTIBLE
TO PARASITIC SPIRITS?

It is complicated to try to explain who are more susceptible to lost souls adhering to their vibratory field, since it is a phenomenon that we cannot see, but we can feel and verify by observing its consequences.

Our task as hypnotists or hypnotherapists should not be to verify concepts or theories, nor should it focus on conducting scientific research on what our clients experience before, during, and after hypnosis sessions. Our task should be to always keep an open mind without being guided by our belief system, that is, by our limitations.

While we cannot provide a scientific explanation about spirits and their ways of proceeding, we can provide statistical information on which we base our concepts. For example, I can say—and without fear of being wrong—that people who have suffered mistreatment and sexual abuse during their childhood are more likely to have a lost soul attached to them. I say this based on the cases that I have had.

In fact, I am not the only hypnotherapist who assures the same. If we follow the work of Aurelio Mejía or read the texts of José Luis Cabouli, we will find exactly the same cases and justifications. Those are our evidences.

Can anyone be susceptible to a lost soul attaching itself to their vibra-tory field? As I mentioned in the previous chapters, in order for a soul to attach itself to our aura, there must be an enabling environment. Anger, despair, and vice are perfect components to create this. For example, I have had clients who had lost souls attached to them while frequenting brothels. In that case, the individual attracted souls who were vibrating at the same level as he was.

So, answering the initial question, we do not all attract or are exposed to lost souls or different psychic forms attaching themselves to us.

I will list some scenarios in which one might be more prone, keeping in mind that they are only a point of reference for when we conduct the initial interview with our client prior to a hypnosis session. If the client mentions any of these conditions, then we should pay closer attention during the ses-sion in case we encounter parasitic spirits.

- **People Who Abuse Drugs or Alcohol**

This type of substance puts us in an altered state of consciousness in which we have no control or decision-making power over what we are experiencing. Faced with its effects, we can only wait for it to wear off. People who constantly enter this state are totally exposed and defense-less against entities.

On the other hand, there will also be lost souls who decide to attach themselves to a person's vibratory field by identifying with their vices or habits. It is difficult to explain how these souls, who have no body, can feel the effects of drugs or alcohol.

When I have asked those lost souls who have appeared in my sessions why they decided to attach to my clients, they have given me to under-stand that, somehow, they can experience at an energetic level what the body of a person who consumes these substances feels.

- **Ayahuasca, Mushrooms, and Other Sacred Plants**

As I expressed at the beginning of this book, since ancient times, hu-man beings have sought different ways to communicate with spirits; be they loved ones, ancestors, or deities. The chemical components that these plants and roots possess make the person who consumes them en-ter an expanded state of consciousness without any control.

In the case of ayahuasca, the effect can last for several hours and, in that time, the person who ingested it will leave their body. And, if this is so, who will take care of the body?

In a demonstration session facilitated by José Luis Cabouli, during the Past Life Therapy course I attended, I was able to witness a fellow student returning to the event where she was ingesting ayahuasca. She began to relive all the symptoms, explaining that her spirit had left her body without any control. Moreover, she felt that she was going to die in that place and that no one could save her. What she described next was a kind of huge parasite that began to enter her body as she floated above it. Similarly, there are people who have had beautiful experiences.

However, as spiritual sessions with sacred plants have gained popularity in recent times, many individuals have appeared who call themselves trained shamans when, in reality, they are only looking for financial gain.

- **Organ Transplantation**

It is said that every organ has a conscience. That is why, in some of my sessions, I have dared to ask my clients to have a conversation with their heart or liver, which were affected at that moment. To my surprise, they began to dialogue with me and tell me what was happening to them.

Hallucination or suggestion? No one can know. William J. Baldwin, in his book *Spirit Releasement Therapy*, also supports this concept: *Organs and body fluids carry the vital energy of the physical body. They can also carry a fragment of consciousness.*

A case in point is that of my colleague Alba Weinman, who treated a client who had had a failed corneal transplant, as it had been rejected by their body. When she began talking to the cornea, she actually engaged in a dialogue with the spirit of the donor, who did not accept that they had died so young in a motorcycle accident.

It does not matter to prove whether these communications are true or not. If the client feels that it is true and that it is part of their reality and beliefs, then we will treat it as a certainty. What we are looking for is not to verify scientifically what is happening, but to achieve relief of the symptom.

If, during the interview, our client mentions that they have received an organ transplant, it would be good to pay special attention to that area of the body during the session or during the scanning of their vibratory field.

- **Blood Transfusion**

This is a controversial issue, as some religions, such as Jehovah's Witnesses, are against blood transfusions.

One of the references in the Bible is found in Leviticus 17:14:

For it is the life of all flesh; the blood of it is for the life thereof: therefore I said unto the children of Israel, Ye shall eat the blood of no manner of flesh: for the life of all flesh is the blood thereof: whosoever eateth it shall be cut off.

While this passage talks about the sacrifice and blood of animals, the interesting thing is that here it is mentioned that "the life of all flesh is its blood." Based on the same principle about the consciousness of the organs, the blood carries part of the consciousness and vital energy of the person.

This subject was also mentioned by William Baldwin, who maintains that both organs and body fluids carry vital energy and fragments of the person's consciousness. That is why, in an organ transfusion or transplant, part of the donor's consciousness can be transmitted.

- **Trauma and Soul Fragmentation**

I think that one of the most vulnerable stages of the human being is childhood. It is in this period that, because we are small, we are at the mercy of other people and what they do to us without understanding what is happening.

The after-effects of mistreatment and abuse suffered during childhood are usually devastating in most cases, causing depression, anxiety, self-destructive behaviors, bipolarity, low self-esteem, and multiple personality disorder, among other psychological disorders. In addition, during childhood, the critical mind, which is the area that decides what will and will not be stored in our subconscious, is not yet fully developed. That is why everything that impresses us and causes an impact will be stored there automatically.

In the same way, any traumatic experience we go through in our life, whether it is an accident, a rape, or the death of a loved one, will affect us on both a mental and soul level. When we are faced with a traumatic event from which we cannot escape, what is known as soul fragmentation occurs.

What is soul fragmentation? As I explained several pages ago, when we live a traumatic event, there is a part of our soul that, in order not to feel, fragments; that leaves our body and simply goes somewhere else or may even return to the light. This implies that we do not have all our energy.

Since ancient times, shamans believed in the fragmentation of the soul and in the recovery of the soul through a shamanic journey, but, over time, some of us have begun to do so through other techniques, such as hypnosis. José Luis Cabouli, in his book Atrapamiento y Recuperación del Alma (*Entrapment and Recovery of the Soul*), provides information about this phenomenon and the work of healing during therapeutic work.

What symptoms can soul fragmentation cause?

- Feeling of incompleteness
- Feeling of emptiness
- Memory gaps
- Disorientation
- Confusion
- Chronic fatigue
- Difficulty in feeling present

When the soul fragments, it leaves our energy field and aura incomplete. These function as a defense field, as shields that protect us against external energies. If it is incomplete, it is equivalent to being unprotected against those lost souls that seek to attach themselves to us. If the soul is fragmented on multiple occasions, it can produce effects of dissociation in the person.

If the client tells me that they were abused and mistreated as a child or does not remember most of their childhood, I try to pay special attention when visiting such memories. Such was the case with María—in "César's Message"—who experienced all kinds of abuse from her mother and had three spirits attached to her.

- **Entrapment of the Soul**

Whenever our soul was unable to process a traumatic event on a physical, emotional, or spiritual level, part of our energy becomes trapped in that event. It does not matter if it took place during our childhood, birth, in our mother's womb, in a past life, or even after the death of the body in a past life.

This entrapment will not only produce symptoms in our current body, but it will also cause us to not have access to one hundred percent of our soul energy. So, following the principle of multi-simultaneity, which says that everything happens now and at the same time, the entrapment may have occurred numerous times and may be affecting us in our current body.

By not having our vibratory field at one hundred percent, this causes the same impact mentioned in the previous point: lack of protection against external energies, among them, lost souls.

- **Abortions**

There will be times when we will perceive that what the person in trance is feeling is not a lost soul attached. But we must remember that it is not about what we believe and think about our client's sensations, it is about helping them by respecting their inner world and beliefs.

If someone claims to feel a lost soul attached, we do not have to argue with them. The approach should be that, if that is real for our client, we should see it that way too. In other words, if they believe they have a lost soul attached, the process should be followed just as if we were communicating with one.

You may wonder why I have started this section and it is because the subject of abortions is somewhat controversial and there are different points of view about it.

As I have found, a spirit plans their next reincarnation with their spirit guide and group mates. They establish goals and contracts with whom they will interact when they reincarnate. In short, the planning of our evolution is detailed and well thought out. Therefore, I find it hard to believe that a spirit, which in turn chooses the body and parents it will have, does not know that this body will not be born or that it will be aborted. And, even more, I find it hard to believe that, because it was not born, it has decided to remain attached to its mother for different reasons.

Let us also remember that, during the first months of the formation of the fetus, the spirit has not yet occupied the body of the fetus. The fetus is simply a biological suit that the spirit will occupy when it is ready.

This is often a controversial topic among regressive hypnosis therapists, because there will be a few who disagree with my explanation, and who argue that the spirit will be in the fetus from the beginning and that it can remain attached to the mother after miscarriage or loss.

The truth is that no one owns the truth and each of us will handle this issue according to our belief system.

So, why do I claim that people who have had abortions are likely to have lost souls attached? I have included it in this list because, whether real or imagined, the mother feels as if the lost soul of her son or daughter is there with her.

I have seen many women, who in the past made this decision or were manipulated into doing so, come to my office with a great sense of guilt and remorse. I think it is these emotions that manifest in the abdominal area, making them feel like a lost soul. The same happens with recurring thoughts, which come to take energetic form as if it were a lost soul, causing symptoms in the affected person.

In these cases, I treat that feeling attached to the womb as if it were a lost soul. In the same way, I will communicate with them, I will make them talk to the mother, elaborate forgiveness, and help them to go to the light. As I said above, what is important here is what the person in trance perceives and believes.

- **People Vibrating at a Low Frequency**

Based on the principle that the spirit is energy and that our body has a vibratory field that we call aura, it is essential to understand that when this field is weakened, it will not protect us effectively from external energies.

Apart from the fragmentation of the soul, there is another factor that can cause the same damage: our mood. If we are in a depressed or low mood, our aura will quickly be damaged.

But how can we see the aura? Through a camera for Kirlian photography, we will see the corona effect that is generated in any animate or inanimate object. This machine was invented by husband and wife, Semyon Davidovich Kirlian and Valentina Krisona de Kirlian in 1939. Thanks to it, it is possible to analyze a person's mood and physical state by means of the luminous halo.

Because of the way our state of mind influences our vibratory field, I do not recommend facilitating hypnosis sessions when we are not feeling physically or emotionally well.

• People Near Tragic Accident Scenes

A tragic accident usually means that the death of the individual was instantaneous, causing disorientation of the soul upon sudden disembodiment. This, in turn, can cause the soul, upon seeing itself outside the body and not accepting the death of the body, to attach itself to someone passing by at the time.

Let us remember that a lost soul may have different reasons for wanting to stay in this plane; from not wanting to leave their loved ones unprotected or not wanting to leave without having fulfilled certain goals.

This type of case is also mentioned by José Luis Cabouli in his books and by William J. Baldwin in his book *Spirit Releasement Therapy.*

In this last text, the author had the opportunity to attend to war veterans, who showed all kinds of symptoms caused by the lost souls of their comrades or enemies who had died on the battlefield.

• People Working in Hospitals

Hospitals are the largest repositories of lost souls, because it is there where many people die in different conditions, which can cause confusion to the soul that leaves the body. For example, those who died from a heart attack, in a coma, or anesthetized during an operation, when waking up in the spiritual dimension may not understand what is happening.

When they die, from one moment to the next, people can no longer see or hear them. Just remember my conversation with the spirit of the American cowboy in "A Ghost in the House", who was haunting his own home during my friend Christian's session. Remember the despair he felt when he realized that his wife and children could no longer see or hear him?

- **Ouija Board**

If we stop to think about what a person with the gift of mediumship experiences before learning to use it, we will realize that the most frequent problem they experience is that of receiving spirits that want to communicate with them in their room, causing them great fear because they do not understand what is happening.

I also mentioned that a person in a trance is a potential medium. This means that not only can they have the ability to see spirits, but they could also communicate through them without warning, as happened in "The Firefighter with Amnesia," who did not realize that his body had died.

So, what is it that motivates spirits to present themselves to mediums and to those in a deep trance? Apparently, the knowledge that they can manifest themselves through them, either to transmit a message or to ask for help.

The same thing happens with the Ouija board, which, I think, can function as a magnet that attracts spirits desperate for communication. The problem lies in the fact that, with this tool, we are consciously inviting spirits to share our physical and vibratory space without taking into account their evolutionary level or intentions.

That is why people who are vulnerable for any of the reasons mentioned above will be exposed to them.

- **Pact with the Occult**

These are people who make pacts with occult forces or spirits that vibrate at a low frequency. Today, this might seem uncommon, but the truth is that it happens very often.

There are different motives that lead them to do so. Some may belong to sects where they invoke these entities, others promise things in exchange for favors, such as recovering a loved one or getting a good job.

How many times have we heard of people who seek practitioners of black magic in order to take revenge on an enemy or the current partner of someone who abandoned them. Every pact has a spiritual cost, since they are not only acquiring a karmic debt, but they are accepting a kind of agreement with the spirit that will do the work for them, to whom they will have to give something in return on a spiritual level.

The truth is that, as we will see later in "The Young Woman's Pact," since it is a commitment on a spiritual level, it is not limited to a specific life. That is to say, it can continue from life to life, from body to body, because, for the soul, time does not exist, and the deal is not limited by it.

In these cases, it is essential to know what was said at the time of the agreement in order to help break it and leave it without consequence, freeing the affected person.

The Grateful Mother

Rose came to me with the goal of treating different symptoms she was experiencing. Since childhood, she had faced a series of challenges from her father, and that same pattern was repeating itself with her partner, who would later become her husband and father of her children.

In addition to the great sadness and possible depression from vibrating at a low frequency, she also felt back and abdominal pain, conditions for which the doctors could find no explanation.

One of the memories she returned to during the session was the moment she learned of her mother's death. Rose was not only saddened by her passing, but because she had not been able to be with her during her last days, even though she had always taken care of her.

Rose: I received a call from my aunt saying that my mother has passed away.

Antonio: So, what else is going on?

R: I am in another country and this call is a shock to me.

A: How do you feel?

R: It is painful, very painful. I am very sad.

A: Where in your body do you feel that pain?

R: In my chest, and it goes down.

A: Some people feel pain because they couldn't say goodbye.

R: Yes, she died alone in her home and I was not there.

A: That is what you think from a human point of view, but your mother is spirit. When the body is dying, others come to assist her in the process.

R: Yes.

A: Where you are now, there is no time or space. I want you to imagine that your spirit leaves your body and you fly to your mother, at the moment when her body is dying. When you get there you will be able to see her from above. What is happening there?

R: She is in her bed. She is wearing her pajamas, curled up in a fetal position.

The position her mother was in at the time of her death was giving me a clue to Rose's symptoms.

A: Go to her, for you are spirit. Now, you can talk to her and explain what is going on. She needs to know what is happening.

R: Mom, I'm sorry for not being by your side.

A: No. You are there right now. You are there right now. Why are you sorry? You are helping her.

R: She does not feel me.

A: So, touch her. Let her feel your spirit. Don't feel guilty, or sad for her. She needs to know that her body is dying. Explain it to her.

R: "Yes, mom. Yes," she said conversing with her. "You're going to be fine, yes."

A: What is happening?

R: She's just looking at me.

A: Very good. If you like, hold her hand. Explain to her that what is dying is the body, that she is spirit. And, see if there are other spirits in the room helping her.

R: Yes, Mom. You will always be with me, around me. I see you inside me.

This last sentence gave me a clearer signal to understand what Rose was feeling physically.

A: Tell her everything you've wanted to tell her.

R: I have always loved you. I took care of you. I love you. I don't want you to feel pain anymore. I want you to feel good and happy.

A: Now, help her out of her body.

R: Yes.

A: Is she out already? Ask her if she has a message for you before she leaves for home, to the light. What does she want to tell you?

R: "She tells me to take good care of myself and to be happy. Yes, yes," she said, continuing the conversation with her mother.

A: Do you mind if I talk to your mom for a moment?

R: No.

A: All right, I'm going to count from three to one and you will lend her your mind and lips. Three, two, one. Jane, thank you for the communication. Do you understand what just happened to your body?

Jane: Yes.

A: Now, you are no longer in pain and free. It's time to go home. Could you give me a hand to help your daughter before you leave?

J: Yes.

A: Your daughter had colon cancer, what caused it?

J: "She had a lot of responsibilities. She had to take care of me and her children," Rose's mother replied, crying. "She is a very responsible young woman and never complained."

A: And do you think this manifested itself as cancer?

J: It is possible, yes.

A: Do you think she should take responsibility for herself now?

J: Yes.

A: It's time for her to take care of herself, isn't it?

J: Yes.

A: So, let's bring light to the colon area. Explain to her that she doesn't have to carry that responsibility anymore, those emotions, she doesn't have to be sad anymore. Release her and let her body recover.

J: Yes, Rose, you are free now. Take care of yourself, heal yourself. I'm doing great now. You did everything you could for everyone and now it's time for you to take care of yourself.

A: Are you proud of her?

J: Yes, very much so.

A: Thank you for your help, Jane. One more question, do you see light from where you are?

J: Yes, I see light everywhere.

A: It's time to say goodbye and for you to follow that light. Thank you for your help. Three, two, one. Rose, now you understand where that colon cancer came from.

R: Yes.

A: You don't need it anymore.

R: I don't need it.

A: All right, give your mother a big hug and say goodbye. She will always be with you, but it is time for her to leave and for you to be free of those responsibilities.

And so, Rose's mother departed into the light. Both had the opportunity to say to each other what they could not say to each other at the time.

It is important to highlight two key points during the session, which are linked to the symptoms with which Rose had arrived. First, she felt abdominal pain, like the pain her mother felt at the time of her death. This was evident when she mentioned that her mother was curled up in the fetal position, coincidentally because of this discomfort. Second, Rose told her mother that she saw her mother inside her. What did that mean?

If we put both points side by side, we could deduce that Rose felt abdominal and back pain because her mother was attached to her.

During the session, I felt it was not necessary to ask them to confirm this because the communication was flowing so well. Actually, what I was interested in was to help them say goodbye and allow Jane to go into the light.

The Mutilated Man

Lisa scheduled an Introspective Hypnosis session with me to address various emotional and physical symptoms. Her daughter had given her the session as a gift, as she felt she could find relief from it.

Lisa worked as a nurse in a hospital in the rehabilitation area, but she had also worked with terminally ill patients. This fact made me pay more attention to the discomfort she mentioned during the interview and session.

Near the end of our meeting, I asked her spirit if she thought the work was complete or if there was anything still pending. Immediately, she told me that she felt something in her leg, as if it was being bent.

Antonio: I'm going to count from three to one and you will go to that experience where you feel that with your knees. Three, two, one. You're already there. What's happening?

Lisa: I feel pain from above my knee.

Something made me perceive that this symptom came from a lost soul attached to her.

A: I'm going to take that pain into your mind and you're going to let it express itself. One, two, three. Brother, you can communicate now. Have you been there a long time or a short time?

Lost Soul: Not much.

A: When you had a body, were you a man or a woman?

LS: Male.

A: What happened to you, how did your body die?

LS: I had my foot amputated.

A: Did they cut your foot or did something happen to you?

LS: "My leg. They cut it off," he answered in a sad voice.

A: Did your body die due to the amputation of your leg?

LS: "The body..." he said, unable to finish the sentence.

A: Do you want me to help you remember how your body died?

LS: Yes.

A: Okay, I will count from three to one and you will go to the last time you had a body. Three, two, one. You're already there. What's going on?

LS: I am dying. I'm in a bed.

A: And what is your body feeling?

LS: Cold sweats. I am cold, very cold. I think I have septicemia.

A: And your leg?

LS: It is no longer there.

A: Why did they cut it off? Do you know what happened?

LS: "It got sick," he replied, taking a deep breath.

A: Move to the moment when your body dies and you come out of it. What is it that keeps you from going into the light?

LS: I don't know, I don't see it.

A: I ask you, then, is there anything you need to forgive or be forgiven for?

LS: I was an alcoholic.

A: Do you know how that is considered in the spiritual world?

LS: No.

A: Attacking your body is considered suicide. Do you understand me? That's why you don't see the light. Are you sorry for abusing your body like that?

LS: Yes.

A: Then, from the bottom of your heart, ask for help from the beings of light who help the lost brothers. Tell them that you are sorry. Ask for forgiveness and mercy. You can ask the light, God, and the angels to help you end your suffering. Tell them that you are ready, that you have realized.

LS: "Help me," he said in a pleading voice.

Suddenly, in a relieved voice, he said he saw the light.

A: Before you go to the light, at what point did you attach to Lisa?

LS: "Now, Lisa is laughing," he said, smiling too. "At the hospital."

A: And what symptoms have you caused?

LS: In her leg. Sometimes she feels like it's going to come off.

A: One question, did Lisa help you at some point?

LS: "Yes," he replied with a smile.

A: Does she remember who you are?

LS: "Yes, I have her in my head. I'm fine here," he said, referring to being in Lisa's body.

A: Do you want to apologize for attaching to her?

LS: I didn't know I was dead.

A: Didn't you realize that your body had died?

LS: Lisa doesn't know either.

A: So, now that you understand that your body died and that it's time to go to the light, let's apologize to Lisa. You attached to her when you shouldn't have. Help me take away all those symptoms that are yours.

LS: Sorry, I'll take them.

A: Do you know if there is anyone else there with her?

LS: It seem like it, I don't know. Someone is still holding her hands.

A: No problem. In a little while, I'll work on that.

That part of the session, in which I delve into that other spirit that gave her horrendous nightmares, is in "The Young Woman's Pact," the following story.

A: Then, apologize to Lisa for causing her those discomforts.

LS: Sorry, Lisa.

A: Lisa, shall we forgive him?

L: Yes, of course.

A: Okay, brother, continue on your way to the light and take all your symptoms and energy with you. Follow that light that came for you. Lisa, help him out by wrapping him in a cloud of light. Is he gone?

L: Yes

That day the soul of the mutilated man departed into the light, detaching from Lisa's vibratory field. This is one of the many sessions in which I found lost souls attached to people working in hospitals.

Lisa was the one who had cared for him and, apparently, the spirit felt so well under her care that he had decided to cling to her, even though he was unaware of the death of his physical body.

The young woman's pact

This is another segment of Lisa's session. Lines above, I related that the mutilated man's lost soul let me know that there was something or someone holding her hands.

The interesting thing about this is that, during our initial interview, Lisa told me that she bent her wrists when she slept and that she constantly had nightmares in which she felt several hands pulling her and paralyzing her while she was in her bed.

When the mutilated man's soul departed, I asked Lisa to visualize his body to see if there was anything else attached to it.

Antonio: I want you to look at your body from above. Imagine that you are white light. Tell me what you see in your hands. Is there someone holding you from there?

Lisa: I feel my right hand being held. My left hand has been kind of let go, but my right hand is very well supported.

A: What do you feel you have in that hand? What does it feel like?

L: I am tied to something.

A: Do you think that 'something' has consciousness?

L: Apparently not.

A: See what you are tied to.

L: I am tied to a bed. There is something holding me down.

A: That's right. So, I'm going to count from three to one and you're going to go to that bed. Three, two, one. You're already there. What's going on?

L: I am tied up.

A: Are you a man or a woman?

L: Female.

A: Older or younger?

L: "Middle-aged. My heart is pounding. It's racing," she said, breathing rapidly.

A: And why are you tied up?

L: I don't think I'm in control of myself.

A: Who tied you up?

L: "I think my dad," she answered very agitated and shaking her head from side to side. "My feet are tied up too. I'm tied up," she added with evident desperation, twisting as if trying to untie herself.

A: And, how do you feel while you are tied up?

L: I can't even move my feet.

A: Is there anyone else with you in that room?

L: Dad. I think it's dad.

A: Ask your dad why he tied you up.

L: "Why are you tying me up, Dad? Why are you tying me up? Come on, tell me! Am I bad?" she reproached her father in whispers. "I am bad."

A: He tell you this?

L: "That's what I feel like. I know I'm bad," she replied sadly.

A: Why do you think or feel that you are bad?

L: He says that I am bad. He says I am bad.

A: And, what do you feel?

L: "He's got me tied up!" she said with a different, more aggressive attitude and voice. "I'm tied up. I am angry."

A: Let's go back a little bit and see if you have done anything wrong. Let's see if it's true. Go back to when you weren't tied up yet. Three, two, one. What are you doing?

L: I am in the room. I'm sitting on a blanket and I have a book in my hands.

A: Go forward a little more. What else is going on?

L: I am reading.

A: What does the book say?

L: "I'm trying to look," she whispered back.

A: Look at the cover of the book, what does it say?

L: I think there is a cross, but it is not the Bible.

A: So, what do you think it is?

L: Things they want to teach me.

A: Who wants to teach you?

L: They want me to read that book. I think it's Dad.

A: And, what happens when you read the book?

A: "I start to get out of control and get ugly. I become bad. It's as if something possesses me," she explained while hyperventilating, "as if something enters me."

A: Go ahead. What else is going on?

L: I kill a little boy, but it's not me.

A: Who was it?

L: "Something is in my body and it makes me do things. It's something strong. I can feel it. My hands start to go numb," she tells me desperately, "then it has me and I get sick. Bad!"

A: Go forward a little more. Go back to bed. You're tied up. How long are you tied up?

L: I think a long time.

A: Go to the moment that body dies. Three, two, one.

L: "I feel my chest burning," she says, crying.

A: Are you figuratively burning or are they really burning you?

L: I feel like I'm burning inside.

A: And, on the outside, do you see fire?

L: No. I am tied up.

A: Go ahead. What else is going on?

L: I can't feel my hands anymore.

A: Go to the moment you leave the body.

L: I go out and my body goes numb.

A: Now, I ask you, are you Lisa in a past life or are you with Lisa?

L: I am Lisa.

A: What do you do once you are out of the body?

L: I still feel the ties in my hands.

A: Do you think at some point you made a pact with darkness? With that thing you read in the book?

L: I think so because I am still tied up.

A: I'm going to count from three to one and I want you to go to the moment when you make that pact or agreement with what you are reading. Three, two, one. Go back there, what are you saying?

L: I am you.

A: Is that what you are saying?

L: Yes.

A: And what does that mean?

L: I let it take my body.

A: Who are you letting do that?

L: Something ugly and dark.

A: And, in exchange for what, what do you gain by letting that dark thing take over your body?

L: "I don't know. I'm trying to fight. I don't know," she says, squirming.

A: Go back to the moment before you said that and tell them that, from now on, what you said to them is no longer in effect. That applied to that body and that body is dead and no longer exists. I want you to tell that dark thing that now you are you and no one can control you or grab your hands. You are light and you have free will.

L: They're gone. Let me go. Let me go!

A: Tell them that that body is yours and that they can't go in there.

L: This is my body, stop it!

A: Tell them: I break every pact, every agreement, and every promise.

L: There are no more agreements, no more promises. This is my body.

A: Repeat: from today I am free. Let me go! And, now, I want you to turn on your inner light. Now you are free. That's over now. Go to the moment when you are floating out of your body and go to the light. Tell me if you are already going to the light.

L: I sit upstairs.

A: That's right. With the death of that body, that experience is over forever and none of that will affect you again. We understand that, with the breaking of that pact, that is behind you and it will no longer affect you. Today you are free. Today you are your own person again. You are in complete control of your body and soul.

After navigating that past life, Lisa's session was over.

This was a clear example of how the pacts we make with dark forces or low vibrational spirits can harm us from body to body, following us into other lives. How is that possible? As I explained above, time does not exist. That is, any promise, vow, or pact we make, we are making on a spiritual level and it will be carried by our spirit from body to body, from life to life, causing us problems.

Although the context in which Lisa found herself in her current life, helping terminally ill patients to rehabilitate and die, was different, the shadows with which she had made an agreement in a past life, still had her bound, causing her all kinds of problems. This was the origin of the nightmares in which she felt hands pulling her and paralyzing her in bed.

HOW TO HELP A LOST SOUL GO TO THE LIGHT?

It would be arrogant and incorrect to say that my method is the only effective way to help spirits. At the beginning of this book, we have seen how different cultures hold different beliefs and rituals to accompany the soul that has just left the body to travel its path in the other dimension towards the light.

Since my first encounter with a lost soul in a hypnosis session, I am convinced that I came to this life for the sole purpose of helping my lost spiritual brothers and sisters. They suffer without being able to understand what is happening to them and even ignore that their body has died.

Lost souls, as we have seen through the cases I have shared, cannot see the light for different reasons: because of the resentment they feel; because they do not want to forgive; because they seek forgiveness; because they did not realize that their body died; or because, at the time of their death, they were paying more attention to the sadness of leaving their loved ones, than to the beings of light that were coming to help them.

By giving them a hand from this dense third dimension, we allow them to see that light so that our spiritual brothers and sisters can take them by the hand and guide them forward.

On this subject, Allan Kardec received several responses from spirits in his book *The Spirits' Book* (1857):

What should be understood by a tormented soul?

- "An errant and suffering soul, uncertain about its future, and to whom you can provide the solace it frequently begs for when it comes to communicate with you.".

Is it any use praying for the dead and for suffering spirits, and if so, how can our prayers provide them consolation and shorten their sufferings? Do our prayers have the power to appease the justice of God?

- "Prayer has no effect in changing God's designs, but the soul for whom you pray experiences relief because it witnesses the interest you show in it, and because an unhappy soul is always consoled when it encounters other charitable souls who share in its suffering. Moreover, through prayer you may incite it to repentance and the desire to do what is needed to become happy. It is in this sense that you can shorten its affliction if on its part it contributes with its own goodwill. Aroused by prayer, such a desire to improve attracts to the suffering spirit other spirits, who come to enlighten, console and give it hope. Jesus prayed for the straying sheep. In doing so, he showed you that you are culpable if you do not pray for those who are the most in need.".

These paragraphs describe exactly the intention that should motivate us to help lost souls. A soul in sorrow or lost soul is wandering and suffering, and will seek to communicate with us in search of relief.

People in trance are potential mediums and that is why spirits will be able to communicate with them and with hypnotherapists in search of clarity and relief.

Our selfless desire to help these lost souls, together with their desire to improve, will attract more evolved spirits to instruct and comfort them. Not for a moment should we think that we are alone in this mission, for we are only one link in a long and powerful chain.

At the beginning of the book *Workers of Life Eternal*, dictated by the spirit of André Luiz to Chico Xavier, he tells the story of the beginning of a rescue expedition made up of the assistant Jerónimo, Father Hipólito, and the nurse Luciana.

Before starting the work of our first aid expedition, Assistant Jeronimo took us to the Temple of Peace in the area devoted to assistance services, where a learned instructor would be commenting on the need to work with unfortunate spirits in the lowest circles of spirit life encircling the earth. (...)

I got the impression that nearly the whole gathering was made up of spirits who were genuinely interested in voluntarily helping their neighbor. By the greetings and the words they used, I perceived that in the sanctuary there were large and small groups of spirit servants on different missions with multiple objectives. Some of them were dedicated to aiding discarnate criminals; others to helping distressed mothers who had been unexpectedly reaped by the renewals of death; still others showed an interest in atheists because of their remorse-imprisoned consciences. Others were interested in the physical infirm, in those who were agonizing on the earth, in demented souls with no physical bodies, in the children having problems in the sphere invisible to human eyes, in the disheartened and saddened souls, in varying classes of imbalanced spirits, in lost of the wayward missionaries, in spirits bound to their visceral corpses, and in workers of the nature in need of inspiration and care.

So, shouldn't we also consider ourselves part of this group of servants mentioned by the spirit of André Luiz?

In several of my sessions, my clients in trance informed me of the presence of other energies in the environment in which we were. They could have been lost souls curious or waiting to communicate, but I am sure that we have also been assisted at all times by other, more evolved spiritual brothers and sisters.

Michael Newton, American hypnotherapist, states in his book *Life Between Lives* that the best therapist for a client is not the therapist, but his spirit guide. He also believes that we should channel the guidance and information from the guides to let them work through us.

When assisting lost souls, it is crucial that we understand that there is no formula for this work. We must remember that every lost soul has its own consciousness, ego, and personality. Therefore, we cannot expect them all to react in the same way.

Even so, I have designated eight steps to make this job easier to accomplish.

1. Determine the Location

In a hypnosis session, we will encounter lost souls in different situations and conditions. Some will be attached to the person's aura; others will come to communicate with the person without necessarily being attached; and others will be loved ones with whom we can dialogue using the concept of 'no time.'

Why are we interested in knowing if they are attached or not? The difference lies in the type of problems and symptoms they may cause from the place where they are. If we find a soul attached at the level of the stomach, it is most likely that the affected person has symptoms in that area of the body. And, what I have noticed on several occasions is that, when the body of that lost soul died, coincidentally the pain of its agony was related to that same area.

If we remember María's session, in "César's Message," César was attached to her right foot. When I asked him in which area of his body he had been injured at the time of his death, the foot had been one of the affected parts.

What we must keep in mind is that, if it attached to the vibratory field, it is most likely transmitting symptoms, emotions, and thoughts to the individual to be treated. This is where our investigative work begins, trying to find out how and to what extent the individual has been harmed by this lost soul.

In the chapter "How to Find Parasitic Spirits," I presented the different ways to detect a lost soul in the vibratory field: through spiritual scanning, paying attention to out-of-range dates or meaningless responses, involuntary movements, sudden pains in parts of the body, or finding out if they went to the light after the death of the body in a past life. It is all about being fully connected to the session and everything our client says and does.

It is very important to be patient in the process of communication with a lost soul. We must never disrespect them, treating them as negative beings or demons, and, above all, we must always help them from the frequency of love.

Once detected, we should review our interview notes to see if the client mentioned any pain or condition in that area. But the full story will always be obtained in the dialogue with the lost soul.

One thing that often happens, as it did in María's session, is that we will have to work with more than one spirit at a time. For that reason, what I do is to draw a chart of the human body in my notebook, where I point out the location of the pain, the sex, and name of the spirit if possible.

This allows me to keep a sort of inventory of the souls I am working with so that I do not forget any of them. Once a part comes into the light, I put an arrow on top indicating that my work with it has been completed.

2. Find Out Their Story

Every lost soul has a story and a reason for why it was lost or attached to an individual. In order to learn more about it, I ask a few questions:

- How long have you been with (name of person)?
- When you had a body, were you a man or a woman?
- Were you able to leave the body easily?
- Did you leave someone behind?
- What did you do for a living?
- Did that happen recently or long ago?

The answers to these questions can give us an idea of how long the client has been harmed by the spirit's energy.

On the other hand, understanding how their body died, can give us an idea of the kind of symptoms the victim is experiencing, if they are attached to the client. Although, we have to keep in mind that souls suffer from a kind of amnesia that does not allow them to remember all the details, including how their body died.

We should not pretend that the initial dialogue is fluid, as the soul may resist giving us this information. Many will say that they do not want to talk to us, some will assure us that they will not leave, and others will even demand that we leave them alone.

3. Remembering How the Body Died

If we think back to the types of lost souls I have portrayed in this book, there are a few who voluntarily decided not to go into the light and attach to the person. But there are also others who are truly lost and do not understand what is going on. In this case, it would be soul entrapment. This means that, in the process of the death of their body, something was not processed correctly.

For this reason, I consider it essential to help them remember how their body died and to relive the agony they experienced in order to give them the opportunity to end that entrapment. This will only be possible when they process that moment physically, emotionally, and mentally.

Knowing how their body died will give us a better idea of why they could not go to the light: perhaps they did not forgive someone or themself, perhaps they are leaving someone behind, or did not realize their demise.

Although our goal is to help the client get relief from the influence of the lost soul, it should also be our goal to help that other spirit. You could say that, in a way, we are giving therapy to that lost spirit by using the body of the person to whom it was attached.

4. Find Out What is Preventing Them from Going to the Light.

This step applies both to the lost souls attached and to those who decide to manifest in the session without having any relationship with our client.

For example, in "The Firefighter with Amnesia," the firefighter did not realize he had died until he talked to me. There will be some souls who will remember everything that happened to them at death and there will be others who will only be able to remember with our help. Always keep in mind that what we must find out is what happened while they were coming out of their body and when they finished coming out of their body.

One question I ask as their body is dying and they are ready to start to come out of it is: what was the last thought you were able to think with that brain?

I learned this tool from José Luis Cabouli and I find it very useful, because the answer they give us can be the key to understand the reason for the soul's entrapment. For example, if the answer is "I do not deserve God's forgiveness for everything I have done," it is most likely that they do not want to go to the light, mistakenly thinking that they will be judged there. On the contrary, if the answer were, "I will not rest until I take revenge," assuming that they have been killed for some reason, their intention would be to attach to their enemies out of spite.

As we ask more and more questions, we will better understand the cause of *postmortem* entrapment, but one thing we should never do is to assume the reasons why these souls are trapped or lost. Let us not limit or contaminate the experience with our beliefs and assumptions.

Finally, we can ask the question directly: what is it that prevents you from going to the light? The answer will clarify the situation.

It is in this step where we must try to give them light, make them understand why continuing with their spiritual path is the best option or why they should not continue to adhere to the affected one.

Let us remember that the soul, when it leaves the body and does not go into the light, maintains its ego, personality, and beliefs. It is basically the person without the body. So, if they thought they did not deserve God's forgiveness and is afraid of being judged, it is perhaps because their belief is Catholic or Christian. It is here where we could explain to them that in the light there is no judgment, that there are no good or bad spirits, but some are more advanced than others, or that hell does not exist.

When there is a lot of resentment on the part of the lost soul towards another, I apply the forgiveness therapy once they have understood that, with that feeling and hunger for revenge, they achieve nothing, but rather it is what keeps them trapped in that state and dimension. If the grudge is directed at the person who is the victim of the attachment, then we must mediate between the two to resolve the conflict.

Let us remember that this soul is communicating through the person in trance, who, in turn, is processing everything that the soul is expressing, through his or her mind.

Another common reason why souls decide to remain on this plane is because of attachment to their material possessions. This is the case of those who remain in the house that once belonged to them, harassing and scaring the new tenants because they consider them intruders, when in fact they are not.

Here, the idea is to explain to them that, from the spiritual world, they cannot do anything with the property they had. You can even ask them to go forward in time to see what is happening with the property and to meet the other tenants who will be living there. They will realize that there is nothing they can do about it and that they are simply wasting their time in a property that no longer belongs to them.

5. Determine the Symptoms That They Caused

While this step is best applied to souls that are attached to their victim, there will be times when they may not be, but may still cause other types of misfortunes.

Once we have determined where the soul is located, how their body died and what prevents them from going to the light, I recommend asking them: "could you tell me if you have voluntarily or involuntarily produced symptoms in this person?" While waiting for their answer, we should be attentive to our initial notes to determine the ailments that the client mentioned.

Some souls answer immediately with the ailment or discomfort they are causing, but others do not have this information very clear, so I advise to start listing the symptoms the client mentioned in the interview: "do you happen to have something to do with their headaches, for example?"

I would say that, in most cases, although it may seem complicated, ending the symptoms caused can be relatively simple if we have the help of the soul that causes them. However, there are times when the damage done to the victim is devastating and even irreversible.

When asking the spirits about possession in Allan Kardec's *The Spirits' Book*, the following is explained:

If there is no such thing as possession per se, that is, the cohabitation of two spirits in the same body, may a spirit nonetheless find itself dependent on another spirit so that it sees itself "subjugated" or "obsessed" by it to such a degree that its own will is in some way paralyzed?

- "Yes, and these are the truly possessed. You must understand, however, that this kind of domination never occurs without the participation of the one who suffers it, either through weakness or desire. Epileptics and insane individuals have often been taken as being possessed, but they are in need of a doctor rather than an exorcist."

In the section where we talked about the aura, we mentioned the different layers of the aura, as well as the function of each one of them. To better understand this idea, we can visualize the human body as an onion, with the soul being the center and the layers of the aura being the layers of the onion. So, there will be lost souls that will attach to the outer covering; some that, over time, will penetrate a little further; and, others with stronger and more dominant energy that may reach closer to the center.

The level of influence of the lost soul on the victim depends on the depth to which it has reached. Sometimes the penetration is so powerful that the victim confuses their will with the will of the lost soul. He or she may even feel like two different people at times and have gaps of the moments when the will of the lost soul manifested with greater influence.

6. Determine Vulnerability

Finding out the exact moment in which a lost soul attached and how it happened is key to our work, as it will allow us to know the vulnerability of the affected person so that they can avoid this scenario in the future. It is also our task to raise the client's level of spiritual awareness, helping them to realize the changes they must make in their life because, if not, they will remain exposed to this type of influences.

Let us suppose that a lost soul attached itself to our client while they were visiting a brothel. What would be the use of helping the soul to go to the light if we do not help the individual to become aware of the consequences of their acts and low passions? It is they themselves who will have to break the chains that bind them to such souls.

If the affected person chooses not to work on their vulnerability, the same interested parties could force the return of other lower souls who vibrate at the same level as them.

If we remember the session "The Owner of the Wake," with María, to whom the lost soul of a woman attached during her own funeral, we will realize that the vulnerability was not the wake. This was just the opportunity the soul found to attach itself to María. Her real vulnerability was the repeated mistreatment she suffered during her childhood and the possible fragmentation of her soul, which left her energetic shield weakened.

By finding a lost soul and assisting the client in removing the symptoms, we are solving only part of the problem. We must also help prevent another lost soul from taking advantage of their weaknesses.

That is why this step is fundamental in the therapeutic work, as it will lead us to understand what we should work on with our client once the lost soul or souls have taken their way to the light.

7. Finalizing the Assistance (Forgiveness)

Once we have examined the history of the lost soul we are working with, including the reasons for entrapment, symptoms, weakness, and location, it is time to guide it back on track.

First, they should apologize to the person to whom they caused various problems with their adhesion and for the illnesses they caused voluntarily or involuntarily. Then, I recommend asking the affected person if they forgive the soul they have with them for the problems caused.

If the affected person refuses to do so, we must remember that every victim has been an aggressor before. If we recap María's session, in "The Spirit of a Rapist," in which she could not forgive Raúl for raping her as a child, she only needed to go to a past life where they had been a couple and she had left him for someone else to forgive him. Once she realized that he had also been a victim in a past life, she was willing to forgive.

There will be times when it will be necessary to suggest to the person in trance to look for a past life where they have done something similar. They will more than likely find it, and this will make their forgiveness process easier.

We can make this person understand that forgiveness does not mean forgetting, nor agreeing with it, nor making peace. Forgiving is similar to ceasing the ingesting of poison while thinking that the one who is dying is our enemy, when in fact we are the only ones who are harmed.

Once this is completed, I ask the spirit to begin to detach from my client's vibratory field, taking with it all the symptoms and energy that belong to it. While this is happening, I ask the client to visualize and feel how this energy is detaching so that they can tell me when they feel it is gone.

8. Protection

Even though we know that we have already helped to correct the vulnerability of the individual that allowed the attachment, we must still work on their protection. How is this done? Some people might take this as a suggestion, but those who are familiar with energy work make total sense of it.

To end the session, I ask my client to choose a color. Once the color is chosen, I ask them to visualize how their body is covered with that light, with that frequency of color, starting from the head and ending at the feet.

If our client is familiar with the meaning of the chakras, we can instruct them to harmonize these six energy centers, one by one, as the light moves down their body.

Remember not to use vocabulary with which the person is not familiar, as this may cause confusion. In the same way, it is important not to use elements that are not part of their beliefs, especially religious ones. That is to say, if my client is a Muslim, I will not talk to them about protective angels or the Virgin Mary. Likewise, if I have a Christian client, I will not ask them to ask Allah for protection.

While we guide this energetic cleansing, it is good to reiterate to them that, from this moment on, they are free of any influence and that they will become themselves again.

***

During my hypnosis sessions, I let my clients visit those events where there are pending issues to work on. Some techniques focus on the mind, on the subconscious, but, in my case, I prefer to focus on the spirit, since it never dies and possesses the information of everything lived in all its reincarnations.

Although the Introspective Hypnosis technique begins by navigating sad or traumatic memories from this life, many times people begin to describe a past life to me. How do I know this? Because the age, context, gender, or names of the people present in the scene do not match those of this reincarnation.

When someone moves into a past life, we must navigate it and ask the necessary questions to find out the story behind it. If the spirit went to that life, it is because it knows there is some unfinished business to be dealt with or because that life relates in some way to the current one. Perhaps it is the same lessons or mistakes we may be making in this one.

Navigating a past life up to the time of death of the body will help the spirit understand why it faces this or that situation in this life or why it has certain symptoms.

As I mentioned earlier, there will be times when we will think we are navigating our client's past life, when in fact we are in that of the lost soul attached to them. This happens because the soul feels that the body belongs to them and, it seems, that the questions I ask are directed at them. Therefore, they take action and follow my instructions while putting the person in a trance in a kind of standby.

The Girl at the Party

This was the case of Valentina, who came to me in search of answers to her inexplicable panic attacks and the immense sadness in which she was immersed.

Already in a trance, I asked her to go in search of a sad memory.

Antonio: Valentina, travel in time and space. Five, four, three, two, one. You are already there. In that scene you are remembering, is it day or night?

Valentina: "I'm not sure," she answered in a very soft voice.

A: What do you perceive, feel, or comes to your mind?

V: It is not very clear.

A: Well, but you can use your other senses, hearing, smell, or touch.

V: "I don't know where I am," she said with a gesture of confusion.

A: There where you are, look at your feet and tell me what you are wearing.

V: Slippers.

A: Does the body feel young or adult?

V: Young.

A: Does the body feel male or female?

V: Female.

A: What are you wearing?

V: A dress.

A: How do you feel about where you are?

V: Sad.

Up to this point, I was trying to decipher whether it was a memory of this life or a past one. From the descriptions he was giving me, I could tell that it was a past reincarnation.

A: Start walking and tell me what you see there.

V: "It's scary," she said, breathing heavily.

A: What does this place look like?

V: There are many trees.

A: What else do you see?

V: A lot of people shouting.

A: Are those people close to you or far away?

V: They are running and screaming. I don't know what's going on.

A: What do people call you there?

V: Rosa.

This was confirmation that it was not about this life.

A: How are these people dressed?

V: Like a party. It's dark and people are running around. I don't know what's going on.

A: What else do you hear?

V: People with children hugging. Can't see what's going on. Everyone is running.

A: And, did you go to the place alone or accompanied?

V: Alone.

A: How old are you, more or less?

V: Thirteen.

A: Let's find out what's going on. Fast forward a little bit.

V: "They're shooting and I'm running. I'm scared," she says to me in a very soft voice. "They are killing people."

A: Do you see who is killing people?

V: You can't see his face. I'm running and I can't see. I don't know what to do.

A: What else is going on?

V: The police arrive, but they keep shooting.

A: What do people who went to the party transport themselves in?

V: We are all running. They don't have cars. You can't see anything. It's like a ranch.

A: And, in that place, do you speak the same language that we are speaking right now?

V: No.

A: Do you know the name of the city?

V: No.

A: What else is going on?

V: The police are with them. They are shooting at people.

A: Do the police also shoot?

V: "Yes, they are also shooting people. There's nowhere to hide, there's nothing," she nervously describes the desolate scene.

A: What is happening now?

V: They are catching up with me and I can't run anymore. They beat me with sticks and kick me. They leave me lying there to keep killing people.

A: Move up to the moment when you see what happens to you. Do you recover or does that life end there?

V: That's the end of it.

A: Go ahead until the moment you get out of the body. And, now that you are outside, look down and tell me what you see.

V: My body lying there, bloody.

A: Look at what part of the body has been injured.

V: In the stomach and back.

A: Now that you are a spirit, do you know why they killed the people?

V: For drugs.

A: If you take stock of the life of that thirteen-year-old girl, what do you think you had to learn?

V: Not to be alone and to be accompanied.

Up to here, we navigated the past life, but there was something that called my attention: the stomach pain and the fear, which were the same symptoms that Rosa experienced while she was escaping.

A: I ask you a question, are you Valentina in a past life or are you with Valentina?

V: I am with Valentina.

A: I see, that's what I was thinking, where did you attach to her?

Lost Soul: In the stomach.

A: And why attach to Valentina, Rosa?

LS: Because she is not shy and because, when she gets angry, she says what she feels.

A: And, tell me, those anxiety attacks that Valentina feels, are they hers or are they yours?

LS: Mine.

A: Is it the memory of how your life ended as a child and running away?

LS: Yes.

A: Is that why she sometimes feels short of breath, because you died running and you were short of breath?

LS: Yes.

A: Are the headaches yours?

LS: No

A: Do you know if there is anyone else in her body with you?

LS: I don't know.

A: Can you help me check her body?

LS: Yes.

A: Please check from head to toe.

LS: She has much sadness.

A: Do you know where this sadness come from?

LS: From not seeing her parents.

A: Oh, but we have already explained to her that what died were the bodies of the parents, but the spirit does not die and you are the proof of that. Here you are attached to her. Other than that grief, do you see another energy like you in the body?

LS: No.

A: Very well, then, Rosita, why didn't you go to the light? Have you forgiven those who killed you?

LS: Not yet.

A: But, by not forgiving, we only hurt ourselves thinking that we are hurting the other. Also, I ask you a question, before reincarnating as Rosa, did you know how your life was going to end?

LS: Yes

A: So, it's something that had to happen. Have you realized that you have to work on forgiveness? Besides, by being attached to Valentina's body you are causing her symptoms that are not good for her, although I know they are without bad intentions. Do you want to forgive today those who killed your body?

LS: Yes.

It was in this way that Rosa forgave those who had killed her body and apologized to Valentina for the symptoms she had provoked. As she left, she told her to take care of herself and to enjoy her life and her family.

When Valentina came out of the hypnotic trance, she could hardly remember what had happened in the session.

The Sister Without Eyes

Cindy came to my office in order to find the source of her chronic fatigue and fear of murky water.

While in a trance, she traveled back to an event in her childhood, where she woke up and was shocked to see her sister.

Antonio: Let's go in search of a sad memory. Five, four, three, two, one. You're already there. What's going on?

Cindy: I woke up, but I don't want to see my sister.

A: Why?

C: Because she has no eyes.

A: Your sister doesn't have eyes?

C: "I don't want to see her," she replied, frightened.

A: How old are you there?

C: I don't know.

A: Do you feel you are young or old?

C: I am a girl.

A: And do you know what your name is there?

C: Cindy.

A: Is it day or night?

C: Daytime.

A: Did something happen to your sister? Why doesn't she have eyes?

C: I just cover my face so I don't see her and I go to my mom. My mom tells me she does have eyes, but I don't want to see her because she scares me.

There was definitely something very strange about this scene. Why was she seeing her sister without eyes when she had them?

A: Go back to the moment when you wake up, open your eyes and see your sister. Pause there, what do you see?

C: I don't see it.

A: Why don't you see it?

C: Because now her back is turned.

A: There, where you are, mentally ask that person, who seems to be your sister, who she is. Ask her who she is and what she is doing there.

C: She does not tell me.

A: Do you want to lend her your mind and lips to communicate with me and I ask her the question?

C: Yes.

A: "Three, two, one," I said as I touched her forehead. "Sister, you can express yourself now, can you tell me who you are? Can you tell me how long you have been with her? Are you Cindy's sister?"

Lost Soul: No.

A: Can you say who you are? Because Cindy thinks you're her sister who doesn't have eyes, but her sister does have eyes. So who are you? You know I'm here to help you.

LS: I've been with her for a long time.

A: And what attracted you to Cindy? Why are you with her?

LS: I don't know.

A: Are there any symptoms that you have consciously or unconsciously produced in Cindy?

LS: I don't know.

A: I ask you a few questions, do you have anything to do with her incontinence problem?

LS: No

A: With her headaches?

LS: Yes.

A: Something to do with her back pain?

LS: No.

A: Do you have anything to do with her tiredness?

LS: Yes.

A: And, with her depression?

LS: Yes.

A: And, with her having to sleep a lot?

LS: Yes.

A: Her strong character?

LS: Yes.

Up to this point I knew it was a lost soul near or attached to Cindy's vibratory field. By telling me the symptoms it was causing her, it was most likely attached to her.

A: When you had a body, were you a man or a woman?

LS: Male.

A: What is your name?

LS: "Jorge," he answered in a soft voice.

A: How did your body die, Jorge? Do you remember what it was like, was it a natural death?

Jorge: No

A: Did they kill you?

J: Yes.

A: Who killed you?

J: There were several.

A: Was that a long time ago or a short time ago?

J: A long time.

A: Why were you killed?

J: I don't know.

A: How did they kill you?

J: Beaten.

A: Had you done something to get yourself killed?

J: No.

A: "When did you attach to Cindy?" I asked trying to find out Cindy's vulnerability.

J: I don't know.

A: Do you have anything to do with Cindy's youngest daughter? She says her daughter can see and hear you.

J: Yes.

A: Because Cindy says the little girl wakes up at night and sits up in bed staring blankly. Is that you she's seeing?

J: Yes.

A: So she has the ability to see you?

J: Yes.

A: Jorge, have you realized that you are attached to a body that does not belong to you? I understand that, having suffered that traumatic death, having an unfinished business, and being lost, you have attached to Cindy to take her energy. But, it's leaving her tired. She has to sleep a lot, she's suffering from headaches and backaches and you're passing on your depression to her. Are you aware of that?

J: Yes.

A: Do you want to apologize to Cindy for unconsciously causing that?

J: Yes.

A: All right, let me talk to Cindy. Three, two, one. Cindy, do you realize that we have a lost-spirit brother attached to you? Do you forgive him for inadvertently causing you these symptoms?

C: Yes.

A: "Perfect, I'll get back to him. Three, two, one," I said, touching her forehead. "Jorge, Cindy has already forgiven you. Is there a message you would like to give her?"

J: No.

A: Would you like to go to the light today and continue your evolution? But, before that, do you forgive those who killed you?

J: Yes.

So, requesting assistance from the beings of light, I asked Jorge to detach himself from Cindy's vibratory field and her to cover her whole body with light.

As we have seen in this case, the communication with Jorge's lost soul was not very fluid because Cindy had gone very deep into the trance. When she came out of it, she hardly remembered what had happened in the session, let alone having communicated with Jorge.

FEAR AND PROTECTION

Assisting lost souls has its challenges. There will be certain times when we will feel unable to deal with them and doubt the skills and techniques we are employing.

Some of them will make us feel as if we were talking to a wall, which is very difficult to penetrate to get the information we need. This will prevent us from advancing at the pace we want, when, in reality, this is not about us, but about them. Therefore, we must be patient and go at their pace, respecting their processes.

In the same way that we interact with people of different cultures, levels of education, and belief systems on a daily basis, the same happens when we want to communicate with spirits. There will be some who are more evolved, others who lived in different parts of the world and have different convictions than ours. The interesting thing about Introspective Hypnosis is that we will enter with them into a kind of time machine to visit their previous lives and learn their stories.

Personally, assisting a lost soul is very rewarding. It may not make much sense to many, but, just as I enjoy interacting with other people to exchange experiences and knowledge, I enjoy interacting with discarnate spirits to do exactly the same, while helping them to have a better understanding of their situation and the spirit world.

The golden rule for our mission with them is to do everything with love. This is something that, since the beginning of my practice, light beings communicated to me through my clients in trance: "You must do this more out of love."

Gradually, as I gained experience and understood why they were lost, I realized that the beings of light were right. And love quickly became the main motive for helping my spiritual brothers and sisters.

Self-Protection

Each practitioner of regressive or spiritual hypnosis has their own beliefs and intentions before beginning a session. Likewise, each practitioner has their own rituals and procedures to protect themself before, during and after the session.

For my part, at least at the beginning of my journey through hypnosis, whenever I have learned something from those with more experience, I have always tried to imitate it. So, when I saw that many prayed, put flowers, used crystals, burned incense, sage, or palo santo, I opted to try a little of the same. At first, I burned sage, but the smell was too strong for me. Then I tried palo santo because I liked the smell, but it was too strong for some people. Also, I meditated for half an hour before each session to set my intentions and ask for assistance.

However, then I started thinking that, if I feel I need protection, it is because I think something bad might happen to me. I also wondered what a person would feel when entering my office and perceiving this type of aromas. Some, perhaps, would feel that they are entering a healer's office and others that they are visiting a spiritist.

In other words, would the client be relaxed and comfortable going into a session thinking that they have to be protected at all times? I think not and that we would be sending the wrong message about what we do.

In the same way, what would be the reaction of a spirit if I said I come to help you and guide you with love, but you see that I come with a shield and a sword (my supposed protection) to defend myself in case you want to do something to me? Would this make sense? What message would I really be sending?

So, what is the protection that works for me? Coincidentally, what the beings of light have been transmitting to me for a long time: love.

It is the love with which I help my fellow man, reincarnated or not, that protects me at all times. It is my intention to help them and, in the case of lost souls, that I am not there to throw them out or to disrespect them. When they tell me "you are not going to get me out of here," my immediate response is: "brother/sister, I am not here to get you out. You can stay there as long as you want. I want you to know that you are welcome and that I am only here to talk to you and help you".

What this immediately causes is a change in the energy of communication and a lowering of the guard to start working together. We should never approach a session with fear, much less one where we suspect there is a lost soul attached. Fear will work against us and cause them to react differently, becoming defensive.

What's more, if they detect our fear, they may give us a hard time, making us believe they are something they are not, like a demon or Satan.

Something we should not do either is to approach the session from the ego, that is, believing ourselves to be experts on the subject or superior to others, thinking that we are some kind of 'hunters' of spirits.

Letting our ego control us during a session can be counterproductive. If the session does not go according to what our ego wants, our ego may feel hurt. For example, when a spirit decides not to leave its victim, our ego may feel that we have failed in our work.

On the other hand, we must remember that spirits have access to much of our information through our vibratory field, so they will try to appeal to our ego, flattering it so that we lose the line of work. They may tell us that we are advanced spirits, that we have had this or that past life, or that the color of our energy is special. We should be very careful with that, because not all that glitters is gold. Just remember what is said in the section, "Testing the Spirits," which is found in the previous pages.

Intimidation Techniques of Lost Souls

It is essential not to fall into the game that the lost souls will prepare for us. Some of them will try to use what I call 'special effects' with the intention of scaring and frightening us.

We should not be afraid or follow their lead, as this will cause us to lose our concentration and our intention to assist them.

Among the tactics they may use are: insulting us with the objective of hurting us or attacking our weakest points; making noises or growls to give us the impression that we are talking to demonic entities, when it is not true; changing their voices to be thicker and more terrifying in order to make us believe that they are dark entities; move the affected person's body violently to make us think that it is a demonic possession; show reluctance to be helped; tell us that they were waiting for us, that they know us and/or that they know everything about us with the intention of scaring us; and, make unpleasant gestures and signs with their face and hands as if they were performing some kind of ritual.

Over the years, I have experienced all of the above. I admit that, on more than one occasion, this took me by surprise, but, when it happened, I remembered the teachings of Aurelio Mejía, which helped me to stay focused on my assistance to that lost soul.

Not paying attention to these tactics can be a bit difficult, especially when you are just starting out in this field and gaining experience.

For example, despite having repeated a thousand times in the course I teach that neither demons, nor Satan, nor hell exist, I have heard comments from some students that, at some point, they have encountered a demonic spirit in the session and did not know how to deal with it. When I asked them why they thought it was a demon, their response referred to the tactics mentioned above.

If we think about it, the lost soul achieved its purpose by intimidating the practitioner, who, overcome by fear and insecurity, decided that they could not continue working with it.

A Stubborn and Lying Spirit

Virginia came to her session seeking to understand why she was constantly sad and depressed. She also had unexplained pain in her foot and trouble breathing.

Already in a state of hypnotic trance, she began to navigate what was supposed to be a past life of hers. Asking the corresponding questions, something indicated to me that this life belonged to someone else. Her case is a good example of how to assist a spirit that resists, that wants to intimidate us and that tells us that it does not want to leave.

Antonio: Three, two, one. You are already there. In that memory, is it day or night?

Virginia: Night.

A: What is happening?

V: It is dark.

A: Where are you?

V: I do not see.

A: But, you can feel and hear.

V: It is cold.

A: I want you to touch your body. Does the body feel like a man's or a woman's?

V: "I don't know," she answered regretfully. "I think it's a man. My hands are cold."

A: Feel that cold more intensely. What else is going on?

V: He does not want to talk.

This response did not make sense and put me on alert.

A: Who doesn't want to talk?

V: "No," she said, shaking her head.

A: And who is it that says they don't want to talk?

V: Oh...

A: Have you been there a long time or a short time?

V: "Very long," she answered in a shaky voice, as if he were cold, and then started to laugh.

A: Are you Virginia in a past life or are you with Virginia?

V: I don't know.

A: Let's see, have you been there for a long time?

V: "Yes," she said, laughing and crying.

A: So, what are you feeling there?

V: I don't know.

A: Cry, cry. Are those tears of sadness?

V: Of sadness, yes.

A: In that place where you are, can you move?

V: "No, I can't move," she answered in a desperate voice.

A: Why can't you move?

V: It's something in the hands.

A: Feel your hands, how do you perceive them?

V: They feel cold. A little on the feet, but more on the hands.

A: And who put you there?

Lost Soul: "I don't know! How do you want me to know?" she said, changing her voice and getting upset.

It is at that moment that the lost spirit began to manifest itself as it really was.

A: We can find out. I'm going to count from three to one....

LS: No!

A: No?

LS: No, you can't.

A: I can help you...

LS: "No!" he exclaimed, interrupting me again and laughing, "You can't. You can't!"

A: Ah, but of course. You're right. I'm the one who can't and you are the one who can. I get the point. Who's the one who's tied up there and can't get out, you or me?

LS: "Me," he replied, nodding his head.

A: So who's getting hurt, you or me?

LS: Don't tempt me.

A: I am not tempting you. I'm just asking you a simple and straightforward question.

LS: Let's see, why are my hands cold? You tell me.

A: Well, mind you, I'm not here to guess, because if I were guessing I wouldn't be doing my job. I can guess why your hands are cold. You tell me you are in a dark place.

LS: I'm cold. Yeah, see, I'm shivering a little bit.

A: You have something that is holding your feet.

LS: Yes.

A: I can guess, but what I guess is worthless. What is important here is what you feel. Brother, we have two options: either you stay where you are without being able to move or I help you find out what happened. What do you want to do today?

LS: I don't see anything. I'm just cold.

A: Would you rather I help you or not help you?

LS: "Yes," he replied, bursting into tears.

A: I'm going to count from three to one and I want you to go to the time before you enter. Three, two, one. You're already there. What's happening?

LS: Air.

A: What is happening?

LS: It is dark.

A: Is this the time before you go in there?

LS: "Yes, it's up to my neck," he said, squirming and trying to breathe.

A: What is it that gets around your neck?

LS: I think it is water.

A: And, while the water is up to your neck, what do you feel in your legs?

LS: Cold.

A: What do you feel in your abdomen?

LS: Cold

A: What do the lungs feel?

LS: "Air, I can't..." he answered with difficulty breathing.

A: What does the throat feel like?

LS: I don't understand what's going on.

A: I want you to go back even further, to the moment before that started. Three, two, one. Where are you now?

LS: I am relaxed.

A: What is happening?

LS: I'm walking. There's a fence that's near the water—I want to cry!

A: Cry. I want to understand. Where are you walking?

LS: It's a long stone, like cement. I don't know. There's water. I'm thin and something.

A: And what are you walking around for?

LS: I don't know. I'm looking at the water with the feeling of jumping in and my feet are shaking.

A: So, what do you want to do?

LS: Jump into the water. I am cold and nervous. I suspect that there is life in the water. I jump in, but it's cold.

A: What drives you to take the plunge?

LS: I don't want to live.

A: So, why don't you want to live?

LS: I am alone.

A: What is the first thing that hits the water when you dive in?

LS: My feet are bent. I'm sinking.

A: Let me know if that body dies there.

LS: Yes.

A: What are you watching as that body dies?

LS: I rise up and see my body in the water, but I can't quite leave.

A: What keeps you from going into the light?

LS: Understanding. I don't understand why I did it. I see a woman in white. Wait, I grabbed a woman in white.

A: When you came out of the body.

LS: Yes, I carried her.

A: And who is that woman?

LS: Anahí.

A: Who is Anahí?

LS: "My wife," he answered, bursting into tears.

A: What happened to her?

LS: She drowned. She's wearing white shoes and a white dress. Her body is lifeless, I can't understand!

Up to this point I had been able to decipher that the man had jumped into the water, apparently to save his wife, who had also drowned.

I asked him to go back to find out how it all started and he told me that they were walking hand in hand and she suddenly jumped in. He didn't understand why. When he saw this, he also jumped in to rescue her, but she had already drowned. He saw that he was carrying her out, but what he was seeing, in reality, was his spirit pulling hers out of the water.

A: Now have you understood what happened to you?

LS: Yes, she threw herself off and I went in after her.

A: Do you already know what happened to you?

LS: I drowned too.

When I asked her to ask Anahí why she jumped, she replied that she did it to be at peace. She told him that the boy in blue pants did not allow her to be at peace. The boy she was talking about was Anahí's son, who had also died.

I asked him to let me help her go to the light. She told me that she was rising, but that the child did not want to leave.

A: Now, bring your spirit into the light.

LS: I can't.

A: Why can't you?

LS: I don't want to leave. I'm fine here.

A: But you were with your hands tied?

LS: "No, no, no, no," he replied, interrupting me. "I'm fine here. I said,

I'm fine. Look at me, I don't have to go anywhere, what do you want me to do there? I know this place and I know I'm fine. I don't know if I'll be fine there and I don't want to know anything about that place."

A: I get it. So have you figured out what's going on or not? You told me you had to learn to understand. Have you understood what is going on with you?

LS: I got it, but I don't understand.

A: Tell me what you understood.

LS: That I am at peace here.

A: Look where you are.

LS: I'm in the same place I jumped from.

A: No, sir.

LS: Yes, yes, yes, yes, yes.

A: Your body is there, but your soul is not there because you are talking to me and through whom?

LS: Virginia.

A: You have not gone into the light, which means that you cannot be Virginia in a past life.

LS: Well, no, because I am talking.

A: Right. That means you are attached to Virginia.

LS: "That's right," he nodded, "and I'm not leaving!"

A: And who wants you to leave?

LS: I'm not going to leave because I'm comfortable here with her.

A: You can stay there as long as you want. That's not a problem. I don't want to throw you out, nor am I here to judge you. You said you wanted me to help you.

LS: "And, now I'm going to manipulate her," he said, interrupting me. "I can manipulate her. I'm not going anywhere."

A: I don't want you to leave. Look, you're the one who loses here. You are not at peace there.

LS: I am at peace because I stole it.

A: And, if you are at peace, why were you crying just now?

LS: Well, something gets into me, I don't know.

A: That is not peace. He who is at peace does not cry.

LS: But, I'm cool as a cucumber, look at me. Don't bother me anymore! I'm fine and she's going to be fine. I'm not doing her any harm, or did she tell you I hurt her?

A: No, she didn't tell me that.

LS: "She can't tell you anything because I take care of her. She is already mine," he said, pointing his finger at himself.

A: Ah, very good. So, why don't you take her with you?

LS: It is not her time.

A: Ah, that's what they all say.

LS: Yes, yes, yes, yes, but I am not everyone. Even if she wants me to, I'm not going to leave. She wants me to leave, but I'm not leaving.

A: But, I don't want you to leave. I just want to talk to you. Look, I'll ask Virginia. Three, two, one. Switch. Virginia, do you want him to leave without helping him gain an understanding?

V: No. You have to help him understand.

A: You see, brother, we want to help you here. Nobody is going to get you out.

LS: "You heard her," he said, laughing mockingly. "She told you no."

A: Just as you need understanding, she also needs understanding.

LS: We are going to smile together.

A: Like you were smiling just now? Because I could see you were crying. You tell me you fell and your feet buckled, did you feel pain?

LS: No, just cold.

A: I find it interesting because Virginia has foot problems as well.

LS: "That's me," he replied with a laugh.

A: So, that's what I don't understand. You tell me that you want to give her peace, yet you are making her feel something that is not hers.

LS: It's just that I'm not bad. That's why she has trouble breathing too, because I couldn't breathe in the water.

A: And, the bruises that she has?

LS: From when I fell into the water.

A: Exactly! Look at how many things you cause a person you care for and say you're going to make happy.

LS: But she is alive. It's all right. I'm not going to take her.

A: Virginia says she has sadness and anger. Whose is that?

LS: Mine because life was bad.

A: Look at you, poor Virginia, all that you make her feel. I have to fix this.

LS: "You won't be able to. You won't be able to," he said to me in a mocking tone.

A: I am going to call Anahí right now to help me. Three, two, one...

LS: "No! No!" he exclaimed, interrupting me.

A: Anahí, thank you for the communication, did you realize that you jumped into the water because you were sad about the child?

Anahí: Yes.

A: So what's the name of the man who was with you?

An: José.

A: Why did José jump?

An: He slipped.

A: He says he didn't slip, but jumped behind you.

An: That is a lie, he slipped. He wasn't going for me, he slipped.

A: José, can you tell me if you slipped or fell?

José: I slipped.

A: Anahí, then, José decided to stay there and not go to the light.

J: Because it wasn't my fault. I'm not leaving.

A: José, I am talking to Anahí. Let's go by parts. Anahí, so José doesn't want to leave, he has attached to Virginia and is causing her sadness, anger, pain, and even bruises. Why is he angry?

An: Because he wanted to save himself and could not. He wanted to hold on to something and he couldn't.

A: By sticking with Virginia, what is he missing out on?

An: Of the beauty of life.

A: Why don't we ask for help...?

J: He won't be able to, I told you!

A: Who says so?

J: Well, me! The one who generates everything for Virginia.

A: José, did you want to help Anahí?

J: Well, yes, but then I didn't want to and I fell like a fool.

A: But, notice that while you're there resenting her, she's lost and there's a child who doesn't know what's going on. What do you think you should do? Shouldn't it be your role to help them?

J: It is compassion that I have to learn.

A: Was Anahí your partner or not?

J: Yes.

A: And, what should you do out of love for her? Hide and not deal with what you have to deal with? Let that child stay lost and let her stay confused? What kind of man were you?

J: Worker.

A: And, then, why don't you get to work on helping that woman and child who are lost? Look at all the trouble you are causing three spirits.

J: "Don't scold me anymore!" he said, interrupting me, "I am a man of my word."

A: And, what word did you give Anahí? I will love you for the rest of my life...

J: Well, yes.

A: I will take care of that child, right?

J: Yes.

A: And why don't you keep your promises if you claim to be a man of your word? Why don't you take them by the hand and go to the light together? And, while you're at it, leave Virginia alone.

J: That's a good idea.

After a long dialogue with José, he was able to understand his mistake and get the understanding he needed. He worked out forgiveness with Virginia, collected his energy and symptoms and went into the light with Anahí and his son.

This interaction with José's lost soul is a clear example of how complicated it can be at times to help them find the light. There are spirits that initially resist being helped, that challenge us, tell us they won't leave, tell us to leave them alone, and even mock us as we try to figure out the reason for their entrapment.

The key is not to lose patience, nor the line of therapeutic work. We must remain serene and ask all the necessary questions to find out their story. This can only be achieved by leaving our ego aside and doing it from the frequency of love for our neighbor.

WHAT HAPPENS AFTER RELEASING A LOST SOUL?

The symptoms caused by lost souls may disappear immediately after the soul is removed from the vibratory field of the affected person, but there are cases in which ills and ailments take weeks or months to be completely eliminated.

Depending on the level of influence the soul exerted on its victim and how much it penetrated into its vibratory field, the damage caused may, in certain cases, be irreversible.

Some of my clients have reported changes the instant the hypnosis session ended, after the lost soul went into the light; several have reported feeling as if a weight had been lifted off their shoulders, something that was weighing them down and not allowing them to move forward in life; others have reported receiving comments from acquaintances about the change in their facial expression and how different their energy felt after the session; Many have told me of feeling a great physical tiredness the next day, which is not surprising because of the energetic work done or also because the lost soul worked its emotions through the client's body; and, a few report feeling a great sadness or melancholy, as if they had lost someone close to them.

As the lost soul is no longer attached to their vibratory field, the person who was being affected will notice a change in their way of thinking and behaving. They will feel that they are once again in control of their will, as it will no longer be influenced by that external energy.

It is difficult to determine a standard as to what an individual can experience when freeing themself from a lost soul. The most important thing is that they feel the reintegration of their own soul and total control of their will, feeling free to act and think for themself.

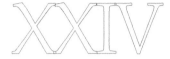

HOW TO HELP US AND HELP US TO OTHERS?

Rebuilding Our Vibratory Field

If I know that I have suffered a major trauma in my life, how can I rebuild or strengthen my aura so that I do not let any spirits attach to me?

The first thing we should determine is what symptoms I have that may lead me to suspect that my soul is fragmented. As mentioned above, some of the symptoms are: feeling incomplete, disorientation, confusion, chronic fatigue, and memory gaps, among others.

But just because we experience some of these discomforts, we should not think that our spirit is fragmented. To reach a better conclusion we should ask ourselves a few more questions:

1. When was the first time you felt this discomfort? This will help us to place ourselves in time, it could be childhood, adolescence, youth, or later.

2. What was going on in my life or what situation was I going through? This will help us locate the event that may be related to the symptom we are experiencing. The event may well have been an accident, an operation with general anesthesia, a scolding from our parents, abuse, rape, or inappropriate touching.

3. What did I feel when that happened? We must analyze what we felt on a physical, emotional, and mental level to have a complete picture of what we experienced at that moment. It could be the sensation of our soul leaving our body, of being frozen in time, of a minute of time seeming like an eternity, of our mind going blank, or of not remembering anything of what we felt.

What we should do next is to ask that part of us to come back, to not to be afraid, explaining to them that it is over. If the event happened at five years of age, we will talk to them as we would talk to a child of that age, telling them that we are going to take care of them, that we have many things to learn together, and that we need them with us to feel complete again.

Then, we can, for example, extend our arms to receive that fragment, taking it to our heart to integrate them back into us. We can decree that, from that moment on, we become one again, feeling complete.

While it is true that sometimes we can do this for ourselves, there are much more traumatic events that have been carried from the conscious mind to the subconscious. This means that, consciously, we do not remember them, but they still affect us unconsciously.

I have worked with clients who, in trance, visited traumatic events of which they had no memory. Therefore, I will always recommend visiting a hypnotherapist in case the discomfort persists after having tried to work through it on one's own.

Detecting Lost Souls in Our Vibratory Field

Can we ourselves do some kind of scanning of our aura even though we are not in a trance? Perhaps during some meditation? Or is there another way to detect these energetic voids?

As in the previous question, the first thing to do is to determine the pain or discomfort that makes us suspect that we have a lost soul attached to our vibratory field. The symptoms that can cause lost souls I have mentioned in the chapter with the same name, but other reasons why we might suspect that we have a lost soul with us are, for example: feeling sad or depressed for no reason, sudden mood swings, thoughts that do not go according to our usual way of thinking, etc.

What we must do next is to place ourselves in the time and space in which this symptom began to manifest itself. What was happening in our lives? What was happening around me with my family and friends?

If, for example, the symptom is a pain in the chest every time I am afraid and we realize that we began to suffer it shortly after the death of our grandfather, who died of a heart attack, then the most logical suspicion could be that the grandfather's soul is attached to us. I am not saying that this is always the case. What I want to demonstrate is the way in which we should think around the symptoms.

So, if we suspect that the grandfather's soul may be with us, what we should do is simply talk to him or communicate mentally with him, and explain to him what happened to the body, helping him to become aware of what happened to him.

Also, let's try asking him mentally what is preventing him from going to the light. Let's see what answer comes to mind. Based on that answer, we can proceed to help him using the techniques I have explained above.

While it is true that we can put ourselves in a meditative or trance state, the truth is that, in order to reach it, our conscious mind must be put aside.

We can try to visualize our vibratory field by ourselves, although the truth is that, in order to start working on it, we must analyze, rationalize, and deduce by asking questions, and joining loose ends; something that is usually done by the hypnotherapist.

Helping the Spirit to Depart

Some spirits lost at death did not see the light. Why did this happen? How can we help our loved ones to die, allowing their spirit to leave the physical body without further resistance?

I think this question applies as much to the moment of our own death as it does to that of a loved one. While it is true that death is nothing more than the transition of the spirit from one plane to another, it is during death that we bring into play our entire reincarnation, the life that is ending.

This is why it is very important to help others and ourselves in the process of death. In the case of our loved ones, it is to help them to forgive everything that was left pending and to ask for forgiveness for everything they believe they did or provoked. In other words, we must help them to settle the pending accounts in this life, since otherwise, they could be dragging them to their next reincarnation.

One of the main reasons for *postmortem* soul entrapment is not forgiving. Either because we may stay seeking revenge, in case someone has done something to us, or because we become victims, in case we do not forgive ourselves for what we did. Whatever the case, the result is the same: the entrapment of the soul.

In the same way, it is fundamental that those of us who are left behind let the spirit of the person who is dying depart. By saying things like "don't leave me," "don't go," "I don't know what I will do without you," or "wait for me to go together," we are not only being selfish, but we are also contributing to the entrapment of the spirit that must go to the light.

On the other hand, it is essential to guide them to become aware of what is happening to their body during the agony. Some people choose to hide from the dying person what is happening to them, that is, that their body is dying. Others prefer to drug them, to put them to sleep so that they do not feel when the moment arrives, which will produce confusion when they awaken in the spiritual world after the death of the physical body.

Let us remember that, during the agony and the process of death, we are assisted by other spirits who have this function. Among these, there can also be our loved ones who have passed away before. Even during the detachment from the body, before death, our soul will gradually gain access to this subtler dimension and we will even be able to see our loved ones and guides. The temperature of the room in which a dying person is in will be lower due to the presence of the energies I mentioned above.

One way in which we can collaborate with the spirits who have come to assist the departing spirit is by not letting our emotions hinder the departure process, as they create a kind of magnetic net over the body, complicating the work of the assisting spirits.

I know it is difficult not to be sad and desperate, but, as much as possible, we must maintain an atmosphere of peace and tranquility, as this is a crucial moment in the transition of the soul. That is why it will always be better for this transition process to take place in a calm environment, such as our home rather than a hospital.

During Pregnancy

How can a mother keep her baby protected from parasitic spirits?

During pregnancy, the fetus and the spirit that will occupy it or may already be occupying it, are within the vibratory field of the mother. Although the spirit that will reincarnate has its own vibratory field, it will be affected and influenced by that of its mother.

Both the mother and the spirit that occupies the fetus have their own lessons, missions, fears, phobias, sadness, and traumas. But, as the spirit of the baby is inside the mother's aura, it will feel everything she feels, both for herself and for her family or social environment.

I could explain in even more detail what the baby's spirit experiences during its time in the womb and all that could harm it not only there but once it is born and begins its life, but, for now, given the topics I touch on in this book, I will focus more on how external energies (other spirits) can affect it.

Pages above, I mentioned who is susceptible to parasitic spirits, I also explained about the holes that are created in our vibratory field when our spirit is fragmented and how it is also weakened when our energy is trapped in traumatic events. Well, all of this also applies and can affect the mother.

Other things that will also influence both her and the baby she carries in her womb will be her behavior patterns and, why not say it too; the places she frequents.

If, during gestation, the mother decides to consume drugs, alcohol in excess, or any hallucinogenic substance that puts her in an altered state of consciousness in which she loses control, her vibratory field will be compromised and weakened. Not only can this affect the baby, but it can also attract lost souls who identify with that behavior, which can attach themselves to her or negatively influence her.

As for places to avoid during pregnancy, I would advise against visiting places that are characterized as large repositories of lost souls, such as hospitals, wakes, cemeteries, or morgues. In some countries, there are museums that used to be prisons, battlefields, or places of torture. I also advise you to avoid them. These establishments are usually damaged not only by the energy stored in them, but also by the lost souls that for some reason or another stayed there.

Within the hypnosis sessions in which lost souls manifested themselves, I have worked with souls that were passed from one person to another at the moment of sexual relations that were maintained for mere instinctive satisfaction and where love was not present. It should be noted that the common denominator in these cases was promiscuity.

For this reason, it is advisable that the mother in gestation, or even the woman before becoming pregnant, be aware that, at the time of the sexual act, we are exchanging energy and frequency. Then, it would be advisable to be aware of who is being allowed to enter the vibratory field.

Lost Souls and Past Lives

Is it possible that I have a lost soul attached to me from a past life?

Yes and no. When we speak of past lives, we are referring to the physical body, to the bodies we have previously occupied. Lost souls do not attach themselves to the physical body but to our vibratory field, to the energy that surrounds our soul. So, under this principle, this is totally possible.

This does not mean that the lost soul goes with us to the light and is attached to us even when it is our turn to reincarnate. Let us remember that lost souls do not see the light. What seems to happen is that they wait for us until we reincarnate to attach themselves again.

Without wanting to believe I am the owner of the absolute truth, since I cannot prove what I have mentioned, I have observed this concept in some of the sessions where the lost soul followed my client from a past life, either to give a message or for a mere settling of scores.

During our lives, are we victims of lost souls that seek to cling to us, without us being able to do anything about it? Well, the truth is that we are not. If we remember what I related in previous chapters, it is not that we are at the mercy of lost souls, but that, in a certain way, by our behavior, tendencies, vices, or addictions, we are attracting them, collaborating in a certain way to this situation as it is explained in *The Spirits' Book* by Allan Kardec.

CONCLUSIONS

When I look back at the road I have traveled in learning hypnosis, I realize that I am not the same person I was a few years ago. Each session with my clients, with the spirits, lost souls, and beings of light has generated a change in me that has helped me to heal my own wounds.

Through them, as they opened their souls to me in search of help, I have learned new concepts. But, for me, the most valuable lesson I have learned is that of love; of seeing beyond the shell that encases our soul, of looking inside each person at a soul crying out for help, as I discovered their identity and found their fragments trapped in other experiences, whether in a past life, in intrauterine life, in early childhood, or in adulthood.

Although, to many this may not make sense, I enjoy communicating with spirits and lost souls. I feel that by helping them out of their entrapment and finding the light, I am fulfilling my life's purpose.

We are in constant contact with other, more subtle dimensions at all times without even knowing it. If we had a kind of spiritual x-ray vision, we could realize that there are spirits everywhere, as if we were sharing the same space, but in another dimension.

In the same way that we have organizations that help the most needy and helpless, the spiritual world has its own organizations or relief groups, whose purpose is to lend a hand to lost souls, both in the process of reincarnation and prior to death. Their task is not only limited to those I have mentioned, but they also help them when they are lost, troubled, or lost in the zone that the spirit of André Luiz calls the 'purgatorial zone.' This means that a lost soul will try to be assisted by these beings of light as long as it is willing to be helped.

Today I can say that I know who I am and what I have come for. I feel that, in a way, I am part of the spiritual relief groups, like many of us who decided to reincarnate to continue evolving, guiding our spiritual brothers and sisters from the crust of planet Earth; from this dense third dimension.

I thank everyone who was open to receive all that I have shared in these pages; the product of my years of experience assisting our spiritual brothers and sisters. My intention has always been to put a little light of understanding in the heart of the reader, helping him to know a little more about that dimension that we cannot see, but that, nevertheless, is full of souls crying for help.

If you, reader, already practice some modality of hypnosis, I invite you to also carry out the assistance to the spirits. As I mentioned at the beginning of this book, our therapeutic work would not be complete if we did not also lend a hand to the lost souls attached to the vibratory field of the affected client.

To those therapists who are interested in continuing with this type of work, I do not wish them luck because it is not a matter of chance or coincidence that they are providing assistance to the spirits. This is a work that requires discipline, dedication, patience, knowledge, and, above all, love and the will to help others. These are simply qualities and conditions that are not found by chance in a person.

I wish that you listen to that inner calling, that spark of light that until today has guided you to help others. I also wish that, as of today, we all see our clients for what they really are: evolving souls asking to be heard, as well as those who are attached to your vibratory field, asking for the same.

GUIDING
LOST SOULS
HELPING SPIRITS RETURN TO
THE LIGHT THROUGH HYPNOSIS

Made in the USA
Middletown, DE
14 June 2021